NO LONGER PROPERTY OF
SEATTLE PUBLIC LIBRARY

D0122164

THIS I
BELIEVE

Previous books published by John Wiley & Sons and Jossey-Bass in the *This I Believe* series, edited by Dan Gediman, John Gregory, and Mary Jo Gediman:

This I Believe: Life Lessons

This I Believe: On Fatherhood

This I Believe: On Love

THIS I BELIEVE

BELIEVE

On Motherhood

EDITED BY DAN GEDIMAN
WITH JOHN GREGORY
AND MARY JO GEDIMAN

JOSSEY-BASS
A Wiley Imprint
www.josseybass.com

Copyright © 2012 by This I Believe, Inc. All rights reserved.

This I Believe® is a registered trademark of This I Believe, Inc.

Published by Jossey-Bass
A Wiley Imprint
One Montgomery Street, Suite 1200, San Francisco, CA 94104-4594—www.josseybass.com

Design by Forty-five Degree Design, LLC.

No part of this publication may be reproduced, stored in a retrieval system, or transmitted in any form or by any means, electronic, mechanical, photocopying, recording, scanning, or otherwise, except as permitted under Section 107 or 108 of the 1976 United States Copyright Act, without either the prior written permission of the publisher, or authorization through payment of the appropriate per-copy fee to the Copyright Clearance Center, Inc., 222 Rosewood Drive, Danvers, MA 01923, 978-750-8400, fax 978-646-8600, or on the Web at www.copyright.com. Requests to the publisher for permission should be addressed to the Permissions Department, John Wiley & Sons, Inc., 111 River Street, Hoboken, NJ 07030, 201-748-6011, fax 201-748-6008, or online at www.wiley.com/go/permissions.

Limit of Liability/Disclaimer of Warranty: While the publisher and author have used their best efforts in preparing this book, they make no representations or warranties with respect to the accuracy or completeness of the contents of this book and specifically disclaim any implied warranties of merchantability or fitness for a particular purpose. No warranty may be created or extended by sales representatives or written sales materials. The advice and strategies contained herein may not be suitable for your situation. You should consult with a professional where appropriate. Neither the publisher nor author shall be liable for any loss of profit or any other commercial damages, including but not limited to special, incidental, consequential, or other damages. Readers should be aware that Internet Web sites offered as citations and/or sources for further information may have changed or disappeared between the time this was written and when it is read.

Jossey-Bass books and products are available through most bookstores. To contact Jossey-Bass directly call our Customer Care Department within the U.S. at 800-956-7739, outside the U.S. at 317-572-3986, or fax 317-572-4002.

Wiley publishes in a variety of print and electronic formats and by print-on-demand. Some material included with standard print versions of this book may not be included in e-books or in print-on-demand. If this book refers to media such as a CD or DVD that is not included in the version you purchased, you may download this material at http://booksupport.wiley.com. For more information about Wiley products, visit www.wiley.com.

Library of Congress Cataloging-in-Publication Data

This I believe : on motherhood / edited by Dan Gediman ; with John Gregory and Mary Jo Gediman.
    p.   cm. — (This I believe series)
  ISBN 978-1-118-07453-4 (cloth); ISBN 978-1-118-22980-4 (ebk.);
  ISBN 978-1-118-22986-6 (ebk.); ISBN 978-1-118-22994-1 (ebk.)
    1. Motherhood. 2. Mothers. I. Gediman, Dan. II. Gregory, John, date.
III. Gediman, Mary Jo.
HQ759.T4475 2012
306.874'3—dc23

2011047025

Printed in the United States of America
FIRST EDITION
HB Printing 10 9 8 7 6 5 4 3 2 1

To Margot Trevor Wheelock,
who was responsible for
This I Believe

CONTENTS

THIS I
BELIEVE

Introduction

In 2011, This I Believe, Inc., published a collection of sixty essays exploring the subject of fatherhood. Now we are pleased to complement that publication with this edition about motherhood. The sixty essayists in this book dig deeply into what one writer calls the "definitive relation." When we are children, our mothers are the people we most want to impress and make proud. They are the ones against whom we often rebel, and from whom we may draw our greatest strength. For mothers, their children often are the embodiment of their hopes and dreams for the future.

"Birth *is* the beginning of time," says essayist Geeta Maker-Clark. "For me, it is a great metaphor for all that is still mysterious and magnificent in the world."

Adults and young essayists in this book tell us of the life wisdom they learned from their mothers. Maternal knowledge can be passed in a direct conversation when advice is offered—even if it wasn't solicited. Other times, wisdom is taught in a more indirect way. It may be shared through the words of a newspaper clipping stuck to the refrigerator, or in the faces of a faded photograph tucked in a drawer. Instructions for living a good life can even be found in surprising places: a song lyric from the Rolling Stones, a Beatles album cover, or a timeworn recipe card.

These writers detail the many jobs mothers perform: the breadwinners, the teachers, the cheerleaders, the eternal optimists in a world full of bitterness and uncertainty. We hear about alpha moms, hero moms, and household CEOs. Perhaps the most common role, though, is as the person providing safe harbor from the storms of life. "I remember the security and warmth I felt with my mother's arms around me, knowing that someone was there to focus genuine love and healing attention on my miserable and needy twelve-year-old self," writes Lily Llamzon Darais.

Of course the mother-child relationship—like any relationship—is not always perfect. The bond can be as painful and dysfunctional as it can be nurturing and constructive.

"I know my mother loves me, but I also know it's because she has to," writes Jamie Lemke-Barrand of her battles with her mother. The challenges of intimacy are evident in several essays in this collection, as the writers honestly share their stories of making peace with the mistakes they've made, and of the reconciliations they've struggled to achieve.

The children featured in this collection—both those still in the blush of youth and those recalling their younger days—offer their perspectives on the women who raised them, whether they're biological mothers, stepmoms, or adoptive ones. Even while serving a jail sentence, Michael Taylor drew inspiration from his mother: "Through every obstacle I encountered I would think to myself, 'If Mother overcame her challenges, I have no excuse not to do the same.'" These essayists remind us that mothers may not share our opinions or approve of all our actions, but they mostly do believe in us—and we believe in them, even if we aren't always able to show it or say it.

The passage of time eventually brings an end to the relationship, sometimes through divorce or estrangement, sometimes when a child is given up for adoption, and, for all of us, when death comes. But even in the pain that comes from the breaking of such a fundamental bond, there is hope. Alice Roche Cody already had one son when she experienced a miscarriage at sixteen weeks, yet she has the fortitude to say, "Grief has made me a better mother."

More often, though, it's the child who struggles to comprehend the passing of a parent. Mary Lou Hurley was a teenager when she lost her mother. "My memories of her are how I learned to be a mother," Hurley says, proving that even after a mother's death, her spirit can remain a presence that provides encouragement and guidance through the veil of memory.

"I believe that being a mother is more than biology," advises Jennifer Smith. "Being a mother is a state of mind." In many cases this is a state of resilience and loyalty, the fierce determination of a mother to protect her child. You will read about women who will not give up when the odds are stacked against them, from fighting poverty or drug addiction to becoming a teen mother and raising a child alone. Whether she is a mother hearing her child's diagnosis of autism or Down syndrome, or a child who becomes the caregiver for an ailing mother, these essayists offer their testaments to facing challenges and coming through their ordeals stronger and wiser.

Reading the essays in this book feels like flipping through a family photo album. Each page offers another richly detailed snapshot of daily life from the delivery room to the deathbed. These word pictures draw us into a particular moment and encourage us to linger there—perhaps to recall a similar time in our own lives or to contemplate the wisdom that someone completely different from us derived from his or her experience. The stories here are universal, no matter your age, gender, or parenting status. They are celebrations of our common humanity.

"A mother's love can overcome hatred, animosity, and selfishness," says Bruce Rankin. "It has the power to heal an abused heart and body." We are grateful to these essayists for bravely and honestly sharing their most personal stories, perhaps knowing that their words may provide comfort to an unknown mother or child living thousands of miles away, or even generations into the future.

Evolution

LAUREN LEBLANC

I have come to a place not so much of peace but of understanding.

Once upon a time, I had delusions of grandeur. I believed—as many young people believe these days, I think—that I was special, that I was different, that I was set apart. I truly believed that I was destined for richness and fame because of my talent and "specialness." I was going to live the new American dream. I was not going to grow up to be a "normal" person, not just another number in the growing American census.

But time passed. Reality set in, as did age, and my perspective changed. The paradigm shifted.

I am a schoolteacher. I am married to a salesman. We have a baby, a dog, a two-car garage, and a mortgage. Could my life *be* any more normal?

And yet, I am perfectly okay with this.

If I were to have a conversation with my eighteen-year-old self, I'm sure there is a lot she wouldn't understand. She wouldn't get why I'm not pounding the pavement in NYC, working to get an audition or that coveted part on Broadway. She wouldn't be able to accept that I haven't been to a real audition in four years. She wouldn't be able to fathom that my coworkers have never heard me sing.

She'd be curious about the baby, because she hasn't had much experience with babies. She would wonder about my teaching career, probably calling it "pedestrian." She would look around my very suburban neighborhood and accuse me of selling out. If I'd bought a house, it should've at least been in an interesting, eclectic neighborhood with coffee houses and tapas bars on every corner. She'd probably scoff at the corner house in the painfully suburban neighborhood that I now call home.

But I know things she doesn't know. I know of the alchemy of loss. I understand that those volatile college years—both wicked and wonderful—are a mere microcosm of life, like a lens zoomed in too close on one object. Life is so much more rich and complicated and wonderful and terrible than those four self-righteous years in the bubble.

I know what it means to work for love, to not just sit back and let it happen the way it can when you're young. I know about bringing life into the world, and the complexity of emotions that brings: the confusion, the bone-deep exhaustion, the loss of sense of self, the love that doesn't know how big your heart is, so it splits it wide open.

My life is simple. It is small, and it may seem interchangeable with so many other lives out there. I may never make an impact outside my house, my community, my hometown.

But I've learned that importance is relative. Because to a small few, I am irreplaceable.

When my little girl cries, she calls for "Mama." When she reaches out, it's for me, and me alone.

So, a small life? It's perfectly fine by me. In fact, I think it's what I've wanted all along.

LAUREN LEBLANC is a teacher, runner, crafter, singer, aspiring writer, and native Texan living in Louisville, Kentucky. For three years, she has used the *This I Believe* middle school curriculum in her language arts classes to teach her eighth graders how to put their convictions to paper. She is married to her high school sweetheart and has a three-year-old daughter and another on the way.

Do What You Have to Do

KIMANN SCHULTZ

My firstborn son, the fledgling Marine, called me the other night from a field somewhere in North Carolina. He was cocooned in his Gore-Tex layered sleeping bag, which provided him with the cover he needed to place his forbidden call. It was January, and the bitter cold stretched from my home in Indiana to the East Coast. He and his group had been deposited by helicopter in this field for an overnight exercise.

Daniel told me he had finally learned when he would leave for Iraq and the city where he would be based, although he could not give me details just yet. I asked him how he was feeling about going to Iraq. He said he was okay with it.

If my son is okay with it, then I will be too. Young men like Daniel—partiers, paintballers, road-trippers—simply trade one set of risks for another when they enter the military. At least that's how I've rationalized it. My son's joining the Marines was no surprise: he came of age during the days of 9/11 and the so-called War on Terror.

I then swallow the last vestiges of my humanitarianism. It hurts in my throat, but I need to tell my son this: do what you have to do so that you come back home.

And I will say it to him again and again, even though I don't believe in war or in the politics or the big money that drives it. I believe in art and in learning and in the peace that evolves from these best of human elements. I believe we could better serve humankind with armies of artists, musicians, and teachers, not armed sons and daughters. But my personal beliefs are momentarily suspended, for my son is a brand-new Marine. Duty bound, he will have brothers to fight with, a team to protect, a job to get done. As his mother, I believe in his unequivocal right to do whatever he needs to do in order to survive. When Daniel completes his deployment, I will be ready to absorb any displaced rage and fear, any bit of undigested war he brings back home with him. I vow to see to it that his heart and mind eventually find their way back home as well.

I was driving home from a late meeting when my son called. The moon in my skies lay behind a slight haze, but it shone steadfast and bright, nearly full. I asked Daniel if the moon was out where he was. He said hold on a moment—yes, he could see it too. I told Daniel I was looking at the moon at that very moment and that he and I were making a triangle with our trajectories of sight. The sunlight reflecting off that pockmarked orb was connecting me to my child just as surely as had I put my arms around him. I felt like a navigator and had found my star, and that star had found my son.

Author-illustrator KIMANN SCHULTZ, mother of three, is a first-generation American, the daughter of Ukrainian and German parents. Ms. Schultz currently resides with her husband and songwriting partner, Mike, in Indianapolis, Indiana. Following deployments to Iraq and Afghanistan, Daniel was honorably discharged and is now a student.

Grabbing the Baton

∽

JULIE SELLERS

Tell me the story of me, Momma," my daughter always asks when we snuggle into my great-grandmother's rocking chair at the end of the day.

"The first time I saw your beautiful face, it was nearly covered by a floppy blue-and-white hat, surrounded by a pale blue blanket. All I could see were two chubby cheeks and a teeeeeeny little nose."

"And I looked like a tiny fairy baby?" she asks on a yawn.

"You did, and you weren't bigger than a minute," I always answer. "The nurse handed a tiny little girl to me, and I was so surprised because you felt so light. I thought that if I unwound the blankets, I'd find no baby there at all, only air."

In that instant, I became a mother. I was all alone in a cold room with a stone floor, four thousand miles from home. There was no sterile hospital room, no crying husband—just the two of us. But that moment was just as special, just as magical as if she'd come from my body directly into my arms. From that moment, she was my daughter in every way that mattered.

It's easy sometimes to forget there's another mother out there with whom I share my title, since it seems as though my life began only when I first held my daughter's tiny body close to mine. But my little girl has a history that involved another. Although I might always be a bit sad that I didn't have the privilege to grow Sophie under my heart, I must give thanks to the one who did.

I owe my life to a woman I've never met, who lives half a world away. Her sacrifice gave me all I could ever ask for, and I never forget for a moment that it was her difficult decision—her tears and her pain—that is the foundation on which I've built this life I love.

When my daughter asks to hear her story, I tell her of the floppy hat, the drafty room, and the blue blanket full of air. But as she grows, she will understand that sometimes life is a relay, and you never know who in this world will hand you your baton. It could be someone you've never met, someone who lives a world away, someone you will never be able to repay for giving you the life you always wanted but never dared to imagine you'd have.

I believe the true gifts of our lives come from the most unlikely of sources. If we venture forth with our hearts open, we will always be in the right place to receive them.

JULIE SELLERS is the author of *Immediate Family: The Adoption Option,* a chronicle of her experiences as a single parent who adopted two children from Russia. She has recently published a novel titled *Coming Home.* Ms. Sellers lives in Indiana with her daughter, Sophie; her son, Max; two dogs; one guinea pig; and a turtle.

You Can't Always Get What You Want

KATE SEARLE

The first time my son said "No," he was eight months old and was crawling determinedly toward a temporarily uncovered surge protector. I grabbed him by the hips and restrained him. "No," he cried, nipping at my wrists like a small dog. "No!"

As he dissolved into tears, I understood that I had to hold firm in my denial of the surge protector, yet I felt sorry for him. The knowledge that he would never reach it would disappoint him bitterly. It was then that I realized that a rock song I had heard all my life was the only expression that could possibly convey both firm denial and heartfelt empathy at the same time.

"You can't always get what you want," I sang to him tenderly, using Mick Jagger's cadence but a less insistent tone. Marcus looked surprised, then defiant. "You can't always get what you want," I repeated sadly, almost reverently, like the somber choir that opens that rock classic. Marcus raised his hands to hit my cheeks, and I held them. "You can't always get what you want," I repeated again as his eyes pleaded his case, urging me to relent and let him at the surge protector. I held my ground and moved on to the resolution of the chorus, as a look of profound sadness came over his face.

"But if you try sometimes, you just might find . . . ," I added as he swooned into my chest, finally accepting his loss. "You get what you nee—ee—d."

I had no idea that a Rolling Stones hit would become as much a mainstay of my mothering repertoire as "Itsy Bitsy Spider." The spider song has pleasant and dexterous hand gestures that accompany it, but only Mick has the vital message everyone must learn as he or she grows up.

What has amazed me as I have sung that song dozens of times in the last year is the fact that nearly every time I do it, Marcus becomes a textbook mourner, traveling through Elisabeth Kübler-Ross's five stages of grieving in the thirty-five seconds it takes to sing through each of the three repetitions of "You can't always get what you want" and the final resolution telling the listener how to "get what you need." And I am happy to report that the sad cycle speeds up each time I sing it, with his denial becoming less vociferous, his anger less physical, his bargaining less pitiful, his depression less deep, and his acceptance more complete, allowing him to move on to other things.

My toddler is growing up, reminding me that as much as I may want that cute little baby that my husband and I adopted two years ago, what we both need is for him to grow beyond his babyish ways to the fascinating little boy he is becoming.

Thanks, Mick. I never could have guessed that your words would be such a central part of my parenting.

A Unitarian-Universalist Sunday school teacher, KATE SEARLE lives in Massachusetts with her husband, Curtis, and son, Marcus, and works in administration at MIT. Marcus, now eight, sometimes gets what he wants and usually gets what he needs.

Visitor at the Table

~⊙~

MAYA CHRISTOBEL

When I was fourteen, I painted a picture that is hanging in my mother's house at the end of a long, dimly lit hall. It is a picture of "God" as I knew God back then. He is old, with a long white beard, his eyes diverted by thought or impatience.

I am now fifty-seven. I have to pass this painting two or three dozen times a day walking back and forth from the kitchen to my mother's bedroom—getting her water, her pills, or some forgotten item that would take her half the day to find because she gets distracted by tiny things like lint on the floor. She eventually forgets what she went back to her room to get and yells, "Maya, what am I back here for anyway?" I go to help her remember what she was searching for, not telling her exactly, but letting her discover it on her own, thus salvaging some sense of self-respect in spite of a failing mind.

When I made the choice to return home to live with and care for her, I found an opportunity to move into a flow of life that I had not anticipated or planned. Watching the Weather Channel and *Wheel of Fortune* like clockwork, spending hours dressing and undressing my mother, clipping coupons, taking morning naps that stretched into the afternoon. This became my new rhythm.

One night at the end of a day of tedium, I asked, "What is this all about?" Why have I stopped my personal and professional life to come and live with my ninety-year-old mother in Oklahoma? I got an immediate answer from that deep inner voice I have come to know as Truth, as God, as Spirit, as Love: the voice whispered, "To be fully present with your experience."

So I am now fully present going to the Dollar Store looking for oversized Kleenex that my mother can't live without. Fully present while assisting my mother as she struggles to get out of a chair and plant her feet firmly on the ground, wondering if she can take a step without falling. I am now fully present with my buried childhood memories, and fully present with seeing myself in another thirty years. This daily spiritual practice of being present is what makes room for both compassion and forgiveness to well up in my life with my mother.

Sometimes being fully present feels like a sentence. Like the gauntlet. Like a tall order. But I am doing it. Because I believe that if I am fully present with myself and in the minutia of life with my mother, then I will find the joy and wonder inherent in this passage we call dying. A passage that has us both becoming each other's teachers, helping one another navigate through territory neither of us has ever been.

And my mother and I are not alone on this uncharted journey. Now, "God" is an unmistakable presence in the house, at the end of the hall, not only on the wall, but standing behind me if I fail to get up under the weight of the moment and when I fear I will lose myself and my dreams. I now feel the breath of love around the edges of my life with her. I can faintly smell joy in the air even when this is the time of letting death in the front door and finding a way to openheartedly welcome death and the divine to the table with my mother and me.

MAYA CHRISTOBEL, a psychologist from Harvard University, teaches workshops and classes on rewriting our stories. Her two books, *Freeing Godiva* and *Roadmaps to Success*, were coauthored with Deepak Chopra.

The Power of Parenthood

ANDREA COLEMAN

On a bright spring day nine years ago, I went shopping at a popular store in my small hometown. It was a chore I'd completed hundreds of times before, but this trip was special: it was the first time I took my baby daughter with me.

Kendall was a preemie who, despite being three months old, looked like a newborn. Still, she was alert and active. As happens with babies, alert and active quickly became bored and restless. I picked her up, began the swaying motion every mom knows will calm a fussy infant, and continued shopping.

An older woman stopped and remarked on what a pretty baby Kendall was. She stroked the soft cheek resting on my shoulder and smiled when Kendall snuffled out a tiny snore. As I turned to settle my sleeping daughter back into her carrier, the woman said, "Poor dear, are your hands still too swollen for your wedding band?"

"I'm not married, ma'am," I replied with the respect I was raised to offer my elders.

"Well! You certainly don't look like that kind of girl."

I looked at her over my shoulder, not entirely certain she was serious, only to see her stomp off with an air of righteous indignation. I glanced down at my child, feeling a messy tangle of emotions: surprise, hurt, anger, and, though I hate to admit it, a stab of embarrassment. Until that moment, the idea of anyone assuming that "single mother" and "good mother" were mutually exclusive terms had never occurred to me. As I finished shopping, the woman's words echoed in my mind.

"You certainly don't look like that kind of girl."

As I thought about it, though, I decided to spin her statement in a positive way. Yes, I was a single mother. I was also a good mother. The negative emotions pulling at me began to fade away.

Raising a child alone is as rewarding as it is terrifying, and while I admit it might not be an ideal situation for anyone, it's also not the worst circumstance one can be in. I left an unhealthy relationship when I learned I was pregnant. I would never subject my child to the pain that relationship brought me. I made a conscious decision to be a single mother. It was the right decision, even if some people don't agree with it.

I believe single parents have to be strong, determined, and able to depend on themselves. We must be both mother and father, and undertake both roles with equal commitment. I am now married to a man who is a wonderful father to Kendall, but I wouldn't change the early years when it was just my daughter and me, because I know wedding bands and marriage vows are no guarantee a woman will be a good mother, just as the lack of them is no sign she isn't.

I believe in the power of parenthood—even when the power comes from a solitary source.

ANDREA COLEMAN teaches language arts at Johnson County Middle School in Paintsville, Kentucky. She also writes fiction for young adults and is pursuing her MFA in creative writing. Her greatest accomplishment in life, Kendall James, is the inspiration for everything she does.

Call Your Mother

SUZANNE BIEMILLER

I believe in calling your mother. No matter where you are, no matter what you are doing, a phone call to your mother will make the world seem less daunting and help you feel stronger.

I started phoning my mother in college when distance suddenly necessitated that form of communication. Since then we have been talking on the phone regularly, even though we now live in the same city. We've talked about life's big issues—should I leave a long-term boyfriend and move to another town? Can I be a good mother and work full-time at a job that I also love? When she and my father separated, our roles reversed for a while, as I listened to her questions and tried to help her articulate answers.

But most of the time, we talk about the little things. What did you do today? How is work? Are the girls well? In over twenty-five years of phone calls, certain themes have emerged. "Go outside and look at the moon, sweetie," she'll say over the phone at least a few times a year. "I've never seen it brighter." "I went to the Reading Terminal this morning; the peaches are in." "I'm so proud of you." "I love you."

A few summers ago, some friends from college got together for a long weekend to celebrate our fortieth birthdays. One of the women had been diagnosed with cancer that past winter. Kerry had finished her chemotherapy; her hair was growing back in, and color was returning to her cheeks. Although she was a little more tired than the rest of us, she looked great.

One afternoon while she was napping, the house phone rang. I answered.

"Hello," a young girl's voice said. "Is Kerry there, please?"

"Hi," I replied, "is this her daughter?"

"Yes, it is," she said quietly.

"She's resting now, but would you like me to wake her for you?" I asked.

"Um, I'm not sure," the girl responded in a small voice that sounded as if it were about to crack. I knew immediately that waking her mother was what she really wanted me to do even if she couldn't say it. She needed to talk to her mother, to hear her soothing, reassuring voice on the other end of the phone.

So wake Kerry I did. She sprang out of bed and went outside with the phone. For about an hour, she sat on an old log in the lengthening shadows of tall pine trees, quietly talking with her daughter—a ten-year-old missing her mother, perhaps fearful that she might one day be gone for more than a long weekend. I don't know what they talked about—maybe nothing, maybe everything—but I know how important that call was to both of them.

When I returned home from that weekend, I phoned my own mother. I don't remember what we talked about, but it sure felt good to hear her voice.

That's what I believe in: the healing, strengthening connections and communications between mothers and daughters. My two daughters are now old enough for our own phone conversations, and I cherish each and every one of them— even when they are about nothing important at all.

SUZANNE BIEMILLER lives in Philadelphia with her husband, Rob MacRae, and two daughters, Caroline and Jane, who help her keep it real every single day. In her spare time, Ms. Biemiller works as chief of staff for Philadelphia mayor Michael A. Nutter.

Fighting for Motherland

SUSAN MONAS

When I was eight months pregnant, a friend looked at my ballooning body and said that if he had to choose between going to war and giving birth, he'd choose war. I was dumbfounded. Perhaps he was so terrified by my body that he believed he had more control as a soldier in combat than as a woman in labor. No woman I know would ever consider that the destruction of life could be preferable to its creation. But many women might argue that giving birth, that laborious process of breathing in and surrendering to the successive and repeated contractions of life, is like death. I believe that a woman's final push of human life from her interior to the exterior world is a profound moment of connection with the wonder of life. I suspect that men who go to war discover what women learn from giving birth: appreciation for the value of life comes with a heavy price.

I see many parallels between war and motherhood. Both require bloodshed, a willingness to sacrifice self, and a duty to surrender to circumstances beyond one's control. There is nothing more heroic than a soldier overcoming an enemy or sacrificing himself to protect his comrades. There is no greater bond than the one between men in trenches. But in the words of another friend, a veteran of two wars, "there is nothing like living through the horrors of war to learn about the sanctity of life." This is war's tragic lesson: discovering life's meaning comes at the price of losing it.

I am a mother of three. I too know about sacrifice and surrender to a cause greater than myself. I salute the heroic women living in the trenches every day to protect and preserve life. Women practice dying all the time for their children's sake. While giving birth, they come close to death; in child rearing, they lose their identity to give birth to another; in letting go, they die a little more inside; and if their children should die before them, their grief has no end.

The child I carried for nine months in a body that so terrified my friend is now sixteen. I have told him that if he is drafted, I will volunteer to go in his stead. No one would send a fifty-year-old mother to war, but maybe we should reconsider. If the proximity to one's mortality teaches us about the sacredness of life, then who better understands this than mothers? Imagine a battlefield of mothers. We are trained to defend ferociously, to sacrifice, and to surrender.

We are also the ultimate life givers and recoil at the thought of life-taking. Maybe women don't have the stomach for war, not because we are weak, but because we have borne life—too precious to squander to the capriciousness of war. For what reason did we endure the pain and terror of giving birth if not to revere the creation that began with a first gulp of air and the unforgettable cry of life?

SUSAN MONAS was born and raised in Toronto, Canada, and now lives and works as a clinical social worker in private practice in Seattle. She has three grown adult children scattered throughout three different countries. Ms. Monas has published two excerpts from her memoir *Life on the Border* in *Drash,* a Northwest literary journal. She writes poems and stories about her travels and travails.

My Mother's Gifts

ALIZON KIEL

For several years, my mother was a nurse at the local children's hospital, which included a rotation in their special care nursery. She worked all night and slept when she could during the day. When I was nine years old, she came home and told us she had met "her son." He was a nine-month-old boy abandoned at the hospital. He had a severe birth defect that left him without abdominal muscles, destroyed his kidneys, and gave him bone disease. He had nearly starved to death while living at a nursing home that was ill-equipped to care for him.

She did ask my father, my sister, and me for our blessing, but honestly I don't think she would have listened had we said no. Once we saw him, it was really a moot point anyway: he was amazing!

My mother brought the baby home, and over time she taught him to eat and removed his feeding tube. She helped him learn to walk following surgery to repair his legs ravaged by the bone disease. She gave him the kind of love that not only answers when you cry but anticipates your every need.

My brother is twenty-five years old now and is in cooking school. Cooking school! Still, after everything my mother has done to raise him, she thinks she's "done all right." But if you remind her that she saved a feeble little boy and turned him into a strong, conscientious, kind man, she would say that was in him all along—someone only had to see it.

Yet vision is a gift, isn't it? So are resilience and patience and peace in the face of the challenges she and her children have faced. I have also benefited from her gifts over the years, especially in 2003 when I became pregnant and left a failed relationship. I was an emotional wreck and incredibly afraid when I got a phone call from my mother.

"You're coming home," she said.

As much as I hated to admit defeat, I couldn't do this on my own. My mother rallied around me. She went to every appointment with me. She celebrated every milestone. We cried together. And when my son was born, she was my coach. She even retired from nursing to be his caregiver while I worked.

In preschool, when my son was asked to draw his parents, he always included his grandmother. Their bond remains strong today. And the bond between my mother and me is even stronger. She continues to inspire me every day.

My mother will tell you she hasn't contributed too much to the world other than her children. She doesn't believe in her own strength and courage, her own vision of right and wrong. I hate to ever tell my mother that she is wrong, but on this particular point, on this particular day, she couldn't be more mistaken. Even my mother isn't always right.

I believe in my mother even though she doesn't believe in herself.

ALIZON KIEL is an operations manager living in Austin, Texas. She is a poet, painter, digital artist, and the creator of the Van Gogh Complex, an online bipolar artists' colony featuring the works of artists with bipolar disorder.

Monster Juice

~⌒~

LISA TUCKER MCELROY

I never really knew much until I became a mother. I have learned more from my kids than they have from me.

For instance:

I.   There really are monsters under the bed. Maybe they're not hairy monsters, or big monsters, or green monsters. But monsters exist for all of us, and the essence of kidness is admitting that there are monsters right there in the room and finding ways to get rid of them. Closing the closet door? Arranging the pillows just right? Laying a monster trap? I've found that red monster juice and peanut butter placed strategically near the door are guaranteed to snag even the most reticent monster. Oh, yes, and a Sesame Street CD featuring singing monsters will scare away non-singing ones. JUST. LIKE. THAT.

Would that my monsters could be lured away just so easily. But my kids have taught me that acknowledging the monsters, then coming up with a plan, is the first step toward banishing them for good.

2. Even the littlest thing is reason for wonder. You just have to get down low and look at it. A caterpillar in the driveway is a mystery to be solved. How did he get into the driveway? Where are his mommy and daddy? Why can't we keep him inside the house? What kind of butterfly will he be? And how can we save him from that oh-so-terrible fate: being squished by Daddy's car? A caterpillar transplanted from the driveway into a flower bed by determined little hands teaches me to protect, to prioritize, to place value on the simplest acts and the simplest creatures.

3. Warm milk is good. So are macaroni and cheese, Band-Aids on boo-boos, and twenty-leven trips down the same slide. If you like something, do it, eat it, stick to it. A lot. Why not? Why not nap when you feel like it and fit in other things around that, instead of the other way around? Hugs are good. Why hold them back? Unconditional love is

good, if you're lucky enough to have it. Depending totally on someone else is good, because it offers comfort to the dependent person, because it expresses value to the person depended on.

4.   A goal is the reason for growth, not the result of it. Kids don't create artificial objectives and try to reach them; everything they try to do derives from a real necessity to get the job done. My older daughter first rolled over long after the mommy go-to guides said she would, only because she had to get to a spotted octopus toy on the other side of the room. She's reading now, driven by her suspicion for the past six years that I was editing stories as I read them to her—she had to find out for herself which good parts I left out. Me, on the other hand? I had goals for my kids for when they grew up: they'd be cabinet secretaries, ballet dancers, museum curators. I wanted to work toward those goals. My kids? They just want to work toward growing up.

What if I hadn't become a mother? Well, I wouldn't be downstairs before bedtime making monster juice, that's for sure. But I'd still have artificial goals, I'd still be ignoring the monsters in the hopes that they'd go away on their own, and I'd still be backing out of the driveway without checking first for caterpillars.

As for right now? I have to stop writing. Hug time—someone's got a boo-boo that really needs a Band-Aid and a kiss.

LISA TUCKER MCELROY is a law professor at the Drexel University Earle Mack School of Law. She is also a freelance writer, contributing regularly to outlets like the *New York Times'* Motherlode and *Parenting* magazine. She and her husband, Stephen, are the parents of two wonderful daughters, whose adventures and observations inspire her writing. She and her dog-loving family live in the Philadelphia suburbs.

Tell the Children

∽

PATTY DANN

One April evening, when I came home from teaching, the refrigerator door was wide open, and my husband was sitting at his desk staring at the pen in his hand.

My husband, who spoke six languages and was so meticulous that I called him Dr. Footnote, said very slowly, "I know what this does, but I don't know the name for it."

When we learned that Willem had glioblastoma, the worst kind of brain cancer, I immediately called our pediatrician. "I was just told my husband is going to die. My son is three-and-a-half years old. I don't know how to tell him—what words to use."

"Call Sallie Sanborn," he said. "I worked with her at Bellevue. She knows this stuff."

The next wild year, Sallie guided us through a new chapter of our lives, a simple one of a family being tapped by the Grim Reaper.

Sallie said, "One: name the disease. Tell the truth about the prognosis. Two: reassure the children that they didn't cause it. Three: tell them everything the doctors are doing to help. Four: don't hide anything."

After growing up on the wisdom "Don't tell the children" when anything bad happened, I now believe in the importance of telling them.

One day, early in Willem's treatment, a cheerful visiting nurse named Glenn arrived at the house just as I was trying to get our son, Jake, to bed. When Glenn took out a syringe, I held up my hand to stop him, and practically threw Jake into his bedroom so that he wouldn't see what Glenn was doing.

The next night when Glenn arrived, he said, "This time I suggest another way." "Come," he said to Jake, and Jake took his hand. Jake stood right next to his dad, patting the big scar on his head. Glenn steered Jake's little hand, and they gave the injection together.

My son grew up too quickly. Everybody who loses a parent says that happens, but Sallie helped us find the words to describe that "losing." Not that she took away the pain, but she helped us learn the words to say what it was.

And I learned from Glenn how hiding the truth was more upsetting than seeing what was going on.

My son is now nine years old. This year when a dear friend was diagnosed with brain cancer, Jake said to me, "You can talk to the mom. I'll handle the kid." Jake didn't skip a beat. This was something he knew how to do, just like he'd help tie a younger child's shoe.

Last night we were dancing in the kitchen to the Beach Boys while I made dinner. The phone rang and Jake answered it. "No," I heard him say, "No he's not, he died. But my mom and I are here." It took me a second to realize he was talking to a telemarketer.

We're on a strange journey, my son and I, but it's one we all are on. And I believe, now more than ever, in the importance of being honest with children.

PATTY DANN is the author of *The Goldfish Went on Vacation: A Memoir of Loss* and *The Baby Boat: A Memoir of Adoption*. She has also published two novels, *Sweet & Crazy* and *Mermaids*. Her work has been translated into French, German, Italian, Portuguese, Dutch, Chinese, Korean, and Japanese. *Mermaids* was made into a movie, starring Cher, Winona Ryder, and Christina Ricci.

The Comfort in Rituals

CAROL LATHROP

I believe that ritual is a powerful process that gives meaning to different aspects of our daily lives. I am blessed and healed by one special tradition that has been passed down by the women of my family.

When I was a child, Christmas was filled with family rituals, and the holiday didn't really begin until my mother baked Springerle cookies. German in origin, these rectangular anise-flavored cookies were rolled out with a special wooden rolling pin that had picture indentations of flowers and animals that transferred onto the dough.

My mother's Springerle rolling pin was a gift from her mother who also made the cookies, and although anise was not my favorite sweet, I understood at some level that this baking ritual was very important.

A few weeks before Christmas, my mother would stock up on ingredients, including a tiny bottle of anise oil, and then start baking. Flour would fly as she sifted, and I would come closer as she dropped the egg yolks into the beaters of the mixer so I could watch the dough turn a lovely pale yellow.

Although my mother rarely missed a teachable moment, I found over the years that the Springerle process was mostly practiced in silence. Even as a child, I could sense that the steps of mixing, rolling, cutting, and baking formed a special quiet ritual for my mother, and I was absorbed in watching her concentration, patience, and care in rolling out each cookie perfectly. I remember waking to the warm smell of anise filling our farmhouse as Mother baked the sheets of cookies. She put the cookies into tins with a slice of bread to keep them soft and gave them to family and friends as gifts.

After my mother died, I faced my first Christmas without her, feeling lost and sad. My father quietly suggested that I make the Springerle cookies that year. A few days later I found my mother's Springerle rolling pin and a fresh bag of flour along with her handwritten recipe on my kitchen counter.

So I mixed and sifted and cut and baked my cookies. I put them into tins with a slice of bread and gave them to family and friends. The Springerle tradition helped heal my sadness and loss during that first Christmas without my mother.

I believe that holiday ritual is about honoring and respecting those who pass the tradition to us. Ritual promises that something will happen again year after year; its practice is comfortable and predictable. It is the opportunity to link our history and ancestors with future generations. I believe that holiday ritual weaves family together and makes us all—the young and old, the living and dead—timeless for a few moments.

I make the Springerle cookies each year now without a second thought. I can almost feel my mother and grandmother beside me in the kitchen as I follow their recipe. And to my great joy, my two daughters sit across the counter, quietly watching.

CAROL LATHROP, a former educator and consultant, is writing her first children's picture book. She is the third generation raised on the family's farm in Delaware County, Ohio. With daughters Bryn and Darcy, Ms. Lathrop continues to fill the family kitchen with smells from her mother's other recipes.

The Simple Joys of Life

KRIS HANSEN

My assistant was dressed in a pink baseball hat, Winnie-the-Pooh pajamas, a bright orange apron, garden gloves, and two right-footed frog boots. In my jeans and sweatshirt, I felt plain and underdressed. Despite the differences in our uniforms, we cooperated nicely to get the basil seeds planted in the plastic six-packs. I placed the seeds into shallow depressions in the soil, and my daughter patted them gently, singing a quiet lullaby to the tiny flecks.

Watching her crumble the soil through her fingers and listening to her questions about the social needs of seeds in dirt (Do they get lonely?), I wondered if this project would have any lasting effect on her. When she grows up, will preparing soil and planting seeds be something that she anxiously awaits every spring like I do, checking the progress of the daffodils and crocus in her yard to make certain that life is returning to the ground? Will there be any lasting effects on my daughter from this time shared, hovering over dirt on a cold March morning?

We had eight trays to plant, and her attention lasted through five. Unable to resist the temptation of the Lego vehicles her brother was building, my assistant stood up, brushed the dirt off her hands and onto the floor, announcing that she was all done gardening. As I swept up the dirt that her abrupt abandonment had scattered across the floor, I wondered if it had been worth it, investing thirty minutes preparing and cleaning up a project for a shared ten-minute gardening experience.

The answer didn't hit me until hours later, talking with my own mother, a Minnesotan who spends her winters in Arizona. As winter waned and spring approached, her enthusiastic reviews of the desert warmth in Tucson were sounding tired and bored. In contrast, her queries about the progress of my crocus and primrose were pointed, even desperate, too excited for polite conversation. While I was planting basil with my daughter, she was scanning the seedlings in the Arizona garden centers, hedging her bets about which ones would have the stamina to travel north and survive to give her Minnesota garden a jump-start.

We are alike, she and I; we share joy in the first greens of spring, the love of planting, and the satisfaction of growing and harvesting. What I realized is that I learned those things from her. I was learning it when I was four, digging holes with a cast-off trowel in the freshly tilled soil of her garden. And I was learning it during the hundreds of times we walked through the yard, celebrating each pea blossom and tomato as a masterpiece created, a treasure found.

I don't know if my daughter will enjoy gardening when she's my age. She may not be interested at all. But there's a chance that she will find the same quiet joy in a garden that I do.

This I believe: time spent sharing the simple joys of my life with my children—including sweeping potting soil off the floor—is a worthwhile investment even if the end result isn't guaranteed.

KRIS HANSEN is a chemist, cross-country ski coach, amateur gardener, and aspiring writer living in Afton, Minnesota, with her husband and three children. She enjoys spending time with her family and playing outdoors in all of Minnesota's diverse seasons.

The Buddha Bean

BETH CRAWFORD

I was holding my baby girl in my arms when I got the news. My daughter, I was told, is a reincarnated Buddha, come back to teach us all lessons of compassion. At least that's what my mother-in-law said. For months I had been grappling with how to think about this baby. She was my Bean, my Sweet Pea—a whole garden of cuteness—unique and perfect.

Or maybe not so perfect, given her Down syndrome diagnosis. I had spent hours struggling to reconcile my experience of her with all of the deficits that I couldn't see but was told to expect. I had thought of almost every angle on the problem, but I had not considered that she might be a major religious figure. Hey kid, I whispered, no pressure.

Few believe that my daughter is a god, but many think she is an angel, perpetually pure, innocent, and sweet. After her birth and diagnosis, kind people comforted me by echoing the stereotype that individuals with Down syndrome are especially sweet and lovable, happy and uncomplicated. The stereotype may be true, for all I know, but I'd rather reject it out of hand than interpret my Bean's sweetness as yet another characteristic of her diagnosis.

I have resisted the pull to idealize or deify my daughter. I even qualify the seemingly benign, "She's a gift from God!" by adding "Yes, like all children." It is not that I am an atheist; I just believe she is human. She is one of us, after all, and accepting her as one of us means recognizing her shortcomings. But that said, what new mom goes around insisting on her child's imperfections? It's more natural to claim that your baby is special than to argue that she is not.

This is just one of many mental contortions I have experienced since her birth. It's awkward because, in fact, she is special, and not just euphemistically. Her smile, her toenails, the peaceful way she sleeps—these things seem magical to me, and I revel in them as if they were supernatural gifts that no mother ever experienced before. This has nothing to do with Down syndrome.

When my daughter was born, one of my many fears was that raising a child with Down syndrome would diminish my experience of parenthood, that this would be a less joyful kind of mothering. It is not. I cheer her on as now, at six months old, she grows into the person she is going to be. I sigh over the poignancy of moving up to size two diapers, and I applaud her discoveries of laughter and feet.

My Bean is not a Buddha, at least not any more than anybody else is a Buddha. I believe she is valuable just as she is, and that by embracing her humanity, we make the most of our own.

BETH CRAWFORD, an associate professor of psychology at the University of Richmond, lives with her family in Richmond, Virginia. The Buddha Bean is now a kindergartener who loves dance class, strawberry ice cream, and teasing her little sister.

The Bond Between Mother and Child

BETH BEERY

I believe in the bond between mother and child—even when the mother didn't give birth to the child.

I was born to one woman and raised by another. Being adopted has allowed me to explore the mother-child bond in a unique way. I believe that I bonded with my birth mother while in the womb. I believe that all babies do. I believe that I felt a loss when she left. It lingered as a hint of sadness deep inside me.

When I was twenty-four, I searched for and found my birth mother. It was extraordinary. She was happy that I had found her. That hint of sadness was eased as she and her family accepted me as one of their own. My adopted family was excited for me, and it was a wonderful thing having my birth mother and my mom sitting in the same room getting to know one another.

I was thirty-one when my birth mother died. She died the day after Christmas in 1996. It was very painful. I think about her death often. She had end-stage lung cancer and had been on a ventilator. The day before she lost consciousness, I stood at her bedside holding her hand. I told her that I loved her very much. I thanked her for giving me to my parents because it was where I belonged and I knew that. I then kissed her cheek as she cried.

Two days later, her second husband, my two half-siblings, their father, and I took turns saying good-bye as the machines shut down and she slipped away. It was surreal. I was numb. I couldn't even cry there in that hospital room.

I did cry later. I cried hard. I cried when I saw my mom and fell into her arms. All I wanted was my mom. I remember knowing how odd it was that I was being comforted by my mom because my birth mother had died. I felt so sorry for my half-brother and half-sister. They just lost their mom, and I still had mine.

It is a one-of-a-kind connection. The mother-child bond is not necessarily a product of the birth process. It is a product of love and caring, time and commitment, patience and teaching, enjoying the good times and working through the hard times. Solid cords of each intertwine with one another creating a bond that is forever unbreakable.

Yes, I believe in the bond between a mother and her child.

BETH BEERY was adopted at ten months of age, and she was raised in Boulder, Colorado, where her parents still live. Ms. Beery lives in Lakewood, Colorado, with her two cats, and she works as an occupational therapist. She has enjoyed writing for fun since she was a child.

On the Same Page

ROBIN FITZGERALD

I, like many, believe in the power of the written word. But some days, I give more credit to the carefully snipped out one.

Let me explain.

Over the years, I've been the recipient of countless cards and letters from my mother. But it wasn't until my freshman year in college, my first official year away from home, that the envelopes arrived a bit bulkier than a $20 bill and card stock would allow.

Turns out, they were filled with articles clipped from newspapers.

There were L-shaped articles. Articles that arrived taped together, beginning on 12A and ending on 3C. Occasionally, a glossy snippet from a magazine would show up. And then there were the cartoons—where the two-dimensional characters played out some event oddly parallel to my own life. A breakup. A promotion. A depressed cat. Sometimes Mom would even ad-lib a few comic strip bubbles if the sentiment wasn't quite right.

Over time, the articles reflected political viewpoints she knew differed from my own. Once, when I announced my plan to move in with my boyfriend, now husband of eleven years, she sent me an article about the rising rate of divorce among those who lived together before marriage.

It was then that I recognized the role of the article as an objective third party. The perfect way to communicate about the things we didn't want to talk about. I soon found myself searching for articles about multiple sclerosis research and alternative treatments for the disease that was quietly attacking my mother's nervous system. The student had become the teacher.

Thankfully, the paper-stuffed packages weren't always so heavy.

Not long ago, an anonymous envelope arrived at my workplace with nothing but an ad for a beauty salon inside. Wobbly, disguised handwriting circled the golden hair of the woman pictured and read, "You'd look better as a blonde." If the postmark with my parents' zip code hadn't given it away, I'd still be looking over my shoulder.

Today, I eagerly await the next delivery. But I now view each article, meticulously cut out along imaginary dotted lines, as if it were a coupon for one free, shared experience. As if we were both reading and smirking with the same twisted sense of humor, or swallowing hard at some inevitable facts we both have to face.

Maybe that's why I keep them. And feel a sense of loss for any that I crumpled up in a hasty cleaning frenzy or accidentally used as a coaster. There's something comforting and satisfying in knowing that someone is always thinking about you, even while absorbing her daily view of the world.

I understand now, as a mother myself, that you read everything twice: once with your own eyes, and then again through the eyes of your child.

Sometimes you're on the same page. Other times, the fact that you are simply both looking at the same page is enough.

ROBIN FITZGERALD lives in Los Angeles with her husband and two children and works in advertising. Her parents live in North Carolina. Near a post office.

The Real Measure of a Life Well Lived

ANNIE AZZARITI

M_y mother passed away recently. She left behind no awards, no large inheritance, no monuments to achievement as the world might define the total of a person's life. What she did leave my brother, sister, and me were memories of her love, bits of herself that remind us of who we are.

In the dark corners of her bedroom closet or under the paper lining of a drawer, she carefully tucked away her dreams for our future. I found the delicately crocheted infant outfit she had made for my baptism. There were letters and postcards I had sent and she had kept. We found photographs with names and dates and places written on the back, marking holidays and everyday events in our lives. She held on to every piece of jewelry we had ever given her. There were congratulatory telegrams and cards from her wedding day fifty-eight years ago mixed in with our academic awards and milestones in our careers.

Like a find from an archaeological dig, each relic we discovered opened me up to a new way of seeing my mother. Lucrezia Palmieri Azzariti was born and raised in Venice, Italy. After World War II, she started writing a second cousin named Frank who lived in New York. Six months later, they married by proxy, and my mother was soon on her way to America.

We were a traditional Italian American family: Mom stayed home while Dad worked hard to make ends meet. Their lives revolved around what they called their biggest accomplishment, their "three beautiful children." For my mother, we were her purpose. As we grew up, she tenderly wrapped the artifacts of our childhood in her love and packed them away so she could hold them as part of her past until she left them to us as a legacy of ours. For me, finding these treasures decades later brought me back into her waiting arms.

I believe these items of apparently small significance are the real measure of a life well lived. In a noisy world where what's hot and what's not fill our media, these quiet, gentle discoveries sustain us. These small treasures mark her loving contribution to the world, and reflect back to us—both the small "us" of our family and the larger "us" of the world—our source of love for each other.

Few of us can create grand gestures to the larger society. Most of us live our days within a smaller world, one where we have the opportunities to create bonds of love with each other in ways that are quiet and often go unnoticed.

I believe that we shape our world with kindness and love of what we do in the simplest moments every day. It is ultimately what connects us to each other, no matter who we are or where we live. I believe that with each sweet stitch of my tiny baptismal gown, every old photo, and every scrap of paper, my mother was holding a tender place of love for all of us.

After five years of teaching first and second grades, ANNIE AZZARITI decided to teach to a larger audience and wangled a production assistant job in television. She has produced, directed, and written documentaries that tell compelling personal stories about life. Ms. Azzariti lives in Santa Monica, California.

The Courage of One Woman

∽

LIEN PHAM

I believe in the courage to make difficult decisions.

It was through courage that my mother found a way for us to leave a politically unstable country to pursue a future in America. She was a single parent in the war-torn country of Vietnam, struggling to raise two little girls and an aging mother. Hers was a typical story of a woman's dilemma in an impoverished land brought about by years of civil war. But she was different because she had the courage to make a decision that would change all our lives.

Through various connections, she was able to get us passage on a small fishing boat. The plan was to get to the closest country that had diplomatic ties with the United States, where we would apply for political asylum. It was a dangerous plan, one that many had attempted and failed. And those who failed paid with their lives.

Knowing the risks involved, my grandmother urged my mother to leave her kids behind. She reasoned that my mother could send for us when she reached her destination. She explained that it was not wise to risk the lives of everyone in the family on the open sea. My mother, always stubborn, had made up her mind to take us with her. She would not part from us. She vowed that in death as in life, we would remain together. My grandmother decided to stay behind. The three of us left.

Thus began a difficult journey to our new lives. We tried three times to leave before we finally made it to international waters. While cruising in the open ocean, we encountered a pirate ship. By luck and the skill of our captain, we were able to outmaneuver our pursuer. We landed on Malaysia three days after we began the trip. We proceeded to poke holes in our vessel to prevent authorities from making us go back. We stayed in a refugee camp for a year, waiting for a philanthropic organization to sponsor our family in the United States.

We were given permission to enter the country legally as political refugees. When we arrived in the United States, our first meal was pancakes and bacon. To this day, I still remember that first American meal with fondness. We relied on the kindness of strangers—people who agreed to accept the responsibility of helping us get adjusted to life in the United States.

It has been almost thirty years since we made that journey. There has not been a day that passed when I do not think of the courage it took my mother to uproot her family and move us to a place so foreign that we didn't even know where it was or how to speak its language. It was her courage that enabled us to have a future better than what we dreamt of while growing up in Vietnam.

How do you begin to thank someone who gave you not only life but also a future? I hope that my mother knows it is her courage that I most admire and cherish. It is also a quality that I hope to have inherited from her.

LIEN PHAM was born in Vietnam and currently lives in Dublin, California. She works at a biotech firm as a product manager, managing international relationships. She has two boys, Akira and Aiden, who continuously inspire her with their unbridled enthusiasm for life.

The Juice Box Mom

CANDANCE GORDON

Whenever my kids have a party at school, I am the mom who always signs up to bring the juice boxes. It's not because I'm lazy or that I don't care if my kids have a good party. I am just not wired in such a way that I can fashion sandwiches, made on my very own homemade, organic, gluten-free, sugar-free bread, into holiday-themed shapes. Nor can I make centerpieces that are totally precious using nothing but dental floss and a milk carton. And I'm perfectly fine with that, even though it's taken me a long time to get here.

Alpha moms, with their ability to make gourmet meals from scratch, keep a spotless house, and scrapbook every minute of their child's lives, used to intimidate me. I felt that because I stayed home with my kids, I should be able to do those things, too. So when the turkey-shaped cookies I painstakingly decorated turned out looking like little round pieces of poop, or when company stopped by and there were toys strewn from one end of the house to the other because, instead of picking up, I'd been busy cutting my child out of the dental floss he'd somehow managed to wrap around his entire body while I took a shower, I ended up feeling like a failure as a mom. I felt as though I was letting my kids down because I couldn't do the things their friends' mothers did without messing everything up and freaking out.

After many failed attempts at baking and crafting, and many afternoons spent crying over my inabilities as a mother, I finally, rather begrudgingly, resigned myself to the fact that my lot in life is to be the juice box mom. I worked hard to be the best juice box mom in all the elementary school, and, after one of my daughter's class parties, it actually paid off. Her teacher stopped me as I was leaving and said, "Thank you so much for always bringing extra drinks. Sometimes parents forget that younger siblings will also be attending class parties, and they end up being left out because we don't have enough drinks for everyone." I just accepted the compliment, rather than telling her I brought extra drinks because I never could remember how many kids were in the class. But her compliment taught me an important lesson—just because I'm not crafty or overly domestic, I'm not a failure as a mom.

Not everyone is cut out to be an alpha mom, and there's nothing wrong with that. I believe it's okay to be the juice box mom. I may not bake cookies and decorate them to look like something straight out of *Martha Stewart Living*, but I do provide something to wash them down with. And I think that's just as important.

CANDANCE GORDON lives in Texas with her two children, Max and Grace. She is currently pursuing her master's degree in education and is author of the blog Crazy Texas Mommy (www.crazytxmommy.com). Although she has become a better cook since writing this essay, Ms. Gordon says her kids still refuse to let her bring decorated cookies to class.

The Wisdom of Children

PATRICIA BATTAGLIA

I believe we are born as whole and complete beings with an inherent integrity that exists beyond the physical body. Whatever apparent limitations or disabilities we may possess, our hearts and souls are pure and intact. I have carried this knowledge with me from my earliest days.

Mary Beth, my older sister by two years, was a full and active part of my youth. As children, she and I often concocted wildly fanciful stories and scenarios, which we would act out. I saw her simply as my big sis, a cheerful and protective presence among my siblings and me.

Still, I began to sense there was something exceptional about Mary Beth. I recall being three years old, over-hearing my parents speak in hushed tones of concern about her.

It wasn't until Mary Beth was a teenager that we received a definitive diagnosis: autism. That explained much, including why she was bluntly honest and entirely without arti-fice. Negotiating the social landscape has been difficult for her, yet from my earliest days, I have seen Mary Beth's intrinsic selfhood as sound and flawless. I have grown to view everyone in the same light.

I am now the mother of five incomparable people who range in age from teens to late twenties. For me, they are, among many other things, living proof that each phase of life carries its own joys as well as its own obstacles to over-come. I do not see children as immature or incomplete adults. They are utterly and perfectly themselves.

My first child, and at the time my only child, was nearly two and a half when she started speaking in complete sentences. She questioned everything, often in breathless wonder as her understanding emerged.

One cool autumn day we were at a local playground when she noticed the school building behind me and asked about it. I described what a school is and what happens there. She was struck by the concept of a "teacher" and wanted to know more. I explained that a teacher is someone who helps a person learn new things. "Just like I'm a teacher for you," I concluded.

With a nod of comprehension, my daughter said, "Yeah, and like I'm a teacher for you."

A moment of stunned silence on my part followed, as I realized all the ways I had grown by becoming a mother. I knew there was more in store, that I still had much to learn from my little teacher. All I could say was "Yes, you are."

I believe that in her own way, my daughter had a clear understanding of our relationship. I cannot say she was wise beyond her years. She held the wisdom of innocence and wonder that was very appropriate to her age.

When I was young, my autistic sister taught me that an innate wisdom exists all the time in every child. My own daughter reminded me that this wisdom can still catch me unawares and take my breath away.

A homemaker for most of her adult life, PATRICIA BATTAGLIA lives in Rochester, New York, with her husband and two of her five children. She turned to writing as a form of therapy after a breast cancer diagnosis. Ms. Battaglia is now in good health and is still writing nearly every day.

The Gravity of Love

ELEANOR VINCENT

Being the mother of the bride rekindled my belief that no force on earth is stronger than the power of love.

It began as most weddings do. Willowy as a sapling, twenty-six-year-old Meghan walked toward us in a cloud of satin and lace, her dark hair bound up in white ribbons. She joined hands with her groom. Todd stood ramrod straight in his black suit.

Meghan and Todd spoke the vows they had written: "Before our friends and family, I choose you as the One. The One I will love, encourage, and comfort, when life is easy and when it is hard, when our love is simple, and when it is an effort."

My throat closed around a simultaneous sob and shout of joy. It was a moment as fragile and beautiful as the yellow rose I clutched against my heart. Meghan had planned every detail—each centerpiece, black sateen ribbon, and romantic French song. On that June evening in San Francisco, I marveled at my daughter's courage.

I can still picture Meghan as she was fifteen years ago during a crisis point in our lives. On that spring afternoon, I came home to find my little sixth grader huddled in the corner of our sofa, pale and fidgety. As a latchkey kid, she had answered the phone when the hospital called. An emergency room nurse said Meghan's older sister, Maya, had been critically injured in a fall from a horse. Only eleven years old at the time, Meghan shouldered the terrible job of breaking the news to me.

Maya's irreversible coma ended in brain death four days later. She became an organ donor at the age of nineteen. And I became a grief-stricken mother, clinging to the shreds of my sanity and my world. As time passed, my love for both my daughters helped me rebuild my life. Love had given me the courage to release Maya and give away parts of her body to keep strangers alive. Loving Meghan had given me the strength to go on living myself, to grieve, and to heal. Now, as Meghan and Todd exchanged their wedding rings, I saw again that love is the most powerful force on earth. I believe it holds us together even when grief tears our hearts apart.

Ever since Maya died, no family celebration is as it seems on the surface. Loss mingles with hope; the past dances with the present. How do I balance the conflicting emotions? Through love for both of my daughters, a mother's love that spans the gulfs in time and space.

Five years to the day of their very first kiss, Meghan and Todd embraced as husband and wife. "I have a son now," I whispered to myself. Cheering erupted as the bride and groom walked down the aisle. I followed, almost soaring, and a new wave of cheering began. In front of two hundred people, I jumped for joy. Love's gravity brought me gently back to earth. It is what holds me here.

ELEANOR VINCENT is the author of the memoir *Swimming with Maya: A Mother's Story* (Capital Books, 2004). She lives and writes in Oakland, California. Visit her at www.eleanorvincent.com.

A Bountiful Harvest

KATHRINE LEONE WRIGHT

I believe the harvest is all.

My mother lived, for a time, on a farm in southwest Colorado, years before the community became the beautiful ski resort town it is today. Her life, like her mother's before her, was fashioned by what the earth and its animals produced. Even though she eventually moved from that lovely farmland to the city, the harvest stays with her.

Each year, my mother took my little sister and me picking: tomatoes, bing cherries, apples, peaches, and vegetables of all kinds. What we couldn't pick ourselves, we purchased by the bushel from farmers who lived at the edge of the

Salt Lake valley. We'd bring our bounty home, the sharp smell of tomatoes overtaking the car, and leave the baskets in the carport to keep the produce cool and dry until we were ready to can them, or "put them up" as we called it.

The tomatoes were my favorite, best eaten sliced and smothered with ground pepper. The cucumbers, I simply washed and bit into whole. The pickle-sized ones were seeded, crunchy, and especially tasty. And I fondly recall many desserts of cold milk poured over fresh peach slices.

Canning was a major event as we helped my mother with sanitizing mason jars in a big black kettle, boiling the lids in a saucepan, pitting cherries, and preparing the paraffin to set above the preserves. As we worked, she'd tell us stories about her grandparents' dairy farm, the time she fell off a horse, and other more off-color stories that are now family lore. We put up pickles, stewed tomatoes, spaghetti sauce, jams, and jellies, and, oh, how wonderful the house smelled for days from our efforts. And when the plum jelly failed to set one year, we renamed it syrup and poured it over Saturday morning pancakes. Canning was our succulent genealogy lesson.

About a year after I moved to Florida, I found a farm near my house where I could take my children to pick strawberries. Running up and down the rows with my two toddlers, picking the ripest, best berries and gathering them in baskets, I felt connected to my mother's farm-girl heritage, to the land, and to the order of all things that require tending to thrive. The farm sold its "pick your own" operation two years later, and now that land bears luxury homes. Also part of the order of things, I know.

This year, after an overly wet spring yielded a smallish crop in northern Utah where my mother lives, she lucked into two precious bushels of tomatoes to accompany the peppers and onions she had grown in her own backyard. The salsa my mother and sister made tastes like nothing else in this world.

It's late September now; the harvest moon has come and gone, but there's a box of homemade salsa on its way to me in Florida. There's also solace in knowing that these gardens are built on continuance—that soon enough, we'll have another harvest to draw from. And next season, when I teach my children how to make cherry butter, I'll add an extra helping of cinnamon, and a few new stories. I'll make the recipe my own.

KATHRINE LEONE WRIGHT is editorial director for an advertising agency. After obtaining an MFA in creative writing from Florida Atlantic University, she moved with her family back to their native Utah. They recently attempted a first garden of their own, with plenty of tomatoes.

It Takes a Mother's Love

BRUCE RANKIN

As a child, I did not have the love of my biological mother. Everything in life seemed dark and indifferent to me. I allowed hatred and bitterness to dictate my actions. For fifteen years, my life was a fight to survive, and I was a product of these dark emotions that tormented me daily. My life was in chaos, and I was a player in what seemed to be a demented dream that would never end.

After fifteen years of violence, abuse, and poor decisions, I surrendered my independence to the civil authorities who were in charge of keeping abused children.

My hopes were that they could make my life better. But I was not placing my hopes in the right source, because it would take more than regulations and discipline to save my life. It would take the kind of love that only a real mother can give a child.

I met the mother who would show me a real mother's love in the county orphanage for abused and neglected children. She walked up to me and only asked if I wanted to leave the orphanage and live with her family. Although I could see love in her face and actions, my only thought at the moment was getting out of that place and isolating myself from others. After the hurt that I had experienced, I did not trust anyone. I had no concerns for the thoughts, feelings, or emotions of others. My world and life were consumed with the walls I had built around my heart. I was determined to hold on to the anger and resentment that I believed to be my strength.

Later, I would discover that my new mother's decision to take me into her home was more than a physical act of compassion. She called it a spiritual duty. Her actions proved that claim, and my hardened exterior began to soften. She lived her life before me with power. On many occasions I witnessed her prepare food for people who lost loved ones. She also prepared and took food to people who had no food. I have never forgotten these acts of kindness. Although her duties never seemed to cease, she relentlessly set before me an example of love that changed my life forever.

My mother never acknowledged any difference between her daughters and me, her foster son. I can remember many evenings when she would come home tired from working as a registered nurse at the local hospital. She never failed to cook our supper or get us ready for school the next morning. When we were sick, she never abandoned us. She worked every day to make our lives better. I never witnessed such love and compassion in a person. The way she lived her life before me allowed me to turn away from the bitterness and grudges that made my world so dark.

I know that many mothers have contributed to influencing their children in a positive manner, but my foster mother had a tougher task, and precious little time to accomplish it. She had to strip away the darkness that fifteen years of hatred had produced. She had to teach me how to love myself before I could love others. She accomplished her task, and my life today is a testimony to her devotion, faith, and character.

I believe a mother's love has no boundaries. I know firsthand that it has the power to change lives. A mother's love can overcome hatred, animosity, and selfishness. It has the power to heal an abused heart and body. I believe that it takes a mother's love to heal the wounds encountered at the expense of living life. I can attest this to be true, because it was a mother's hatred that made me bitter, but another mother's love that saved me from self-annihilation.

BRUCE RANKIN currently resides in southern Ohio. He wrote this essay to honor his foster mother on her birthday, although it took him four years to actually read it to her.

A Matter of One's Perspective

JOSEPHINE GUIDO

My son came to visit last Friday, and as he entered he said, "This mirror is still a mess. I noticed it when we were here earlier this week. What's the matter? Are you feeling okay, Mom?"

How should I answer? Would just saying, "I missed it" cover my tracks? He grew up watching me wage war against dirty mirrors and blotchy glass of any sort. When I was young, parenting and maintaining a modicum of cleanliness often caused me to obsess and act like a soldier in a battle against household messes.

On Thursday, after I noticed some smudges and blotches on the back storm door, I washed the glass and the frame.

Near the bottom was a brilliant splatter of coffee spots. Immediately, I knew the perpetrator—our daughter is the only one who takes her coffee black. As I wiped, I recalled all the mornings she's hurried out the door, laden with purse, books, and paraphernalia for her commute to university. She's completed her master's and is now moving ten hours away to finish her education. I wiped the coffee stains with sadness, unlike the frustration of past wipes. A change has arrived.

On the handle of the door, there was a spot of blood. It was ugly, but I laughed at it. My husband had smashed his knuckles as he worked like a lumberjack with his new chain saw. It was a minor injury, and he had been unaware of leaving his mark behind as he played a would-be Paul Bunyan. I cleaned the spot and remembered that it was our children who thought we should buy this particular house because the yard "looks like Dad."

Toward the top of the door was a big greasy splotch— leavings from my six-foot-five-inch twenty-nine-year-old. He had sunscreen on his hands and was pushing his way through the door with his body, as he's always done, talking to me as he went. As I stretched on tippytoe to reach the smudge, I realized that I seldom clean his calling cards anymore—he married and moved away at twenty-three, the age of his sister now. Each wipe of the cloth and stretch of my portly torso reminded me of what a dear and lovable person he's always been. How many times did I direct him on how to go through a door without creating work for his mother? Now, I wipe—grateful for the time he took from his wife, three children, two jobs, and new house to come for a visit and check on me.

So, the entry hall mirror? Well, a couple of weeks ago our son stopped by with his three- and five-year-old children, and the rest is obvious. When I look at that mirror, I see the tiny handprints and recall the precious reflections of my grandchildren. Time has moved on, the children have changed, and the five-year-old is now six. Soon I'll clean the mirror, but until that time the entry hall mirror will remain my own private art gallery. My son may find it difficult to understand the subtle changes that have occurred with me. Placing "grand" before the word "parent" has affected my values. I trust, when he reaches the position I now occupy, that he will comprehend what I believe: that all of life, even art, is a matter of one's perspective.

JOSEPHINE GUIDO has spent most of the last forty years keeping a home. She was born in New England, raised in the Deep South, and has lived her adult life in the upper Midwest. Spending time with those she loves is her greatest source of joy.

Putting Myself First

~⌒~

SHERI WEINBERG

Like many, I never paid much attention to the flight attendant's explanation of emergency procedures. After hearing it over and over, I assumed that what I needed to know must by now be embedded into my brain. It never occurred to me that one simple instruction during that demonstration could be applied to my everyday life.

Do you know why the flight attendant tells you that when traveling with small children, you should put the oxygen mask on yourself before your child? The reason is that if you put the mask on the child first, as was my first instinct as a mother, you might pass out before you are able to put the mask on yourself.

I learned this from a recovering heroin addict. After a thwarted suicide attempt, I was admitted to a psychiatric hospital. While in the hospital, my abusive husband of fifteen years coached my two young daughters to tell me that I was "too scary" and that they didn't want me to come home. I was devastated.

The heroin addict was also a mother. During a group session after I related what had happened, she said she knew how I felt, and that she was going through rehab in order to regain custody of her children. She then told us what her counselor had told her about the oxygen mask, and said that story was what gave her the courage to fight for recovery.

This young mother said to me, "It don't make no difference if your kids were told what to say. If you don't fix yourself first, you can't be a good mom." She said I needed to put my girls second and just focus on getting well so that when I left the hospital I could be a good example to my daughters. Whether or not they were scared, I would be able to prove to them that I was OK.

This seemed impossible to me. I had come to believe that I was unimportant, and thought it was too selfish to put myself first. But I kept thinking about the example of the oxygen mask, and it started to make sense.

Four weeks later I left the hospital, and about six months after that I won emergency protective custody of my daughters. Ten years later, I have a remarkably wonderful relationship with two emotionally healthy young women. One daughter is married to a kind and respectful young man, and the other is also in a very loving relationship.

I believe that in order to be a good parent, I must put my own well-being first. I have learned that this is not a selfish attitude, but a way that enables me to effectively take care of my children.

SHERI WEINBERG is a survivor of domestic violence. Her interests include reading, writing, fine arts, cooking, baking, domestic violence advocacy, and mental health advocacy. She has two daughters, one son-in-law, and three grandsons.

Listen to Your Mother-in-Law

❧

JUDI RUSSELL

When I was a newlywed thirty-seven years ago, my husband gave me a lacey, shell-colored nightgown. I told my mother-in-law the gown was far too beautiful to use every day, that I'd save it for special occasions.

My mother-in-law gave me some good advice: "Wear the nightgown. Just think of all the things people were saving for special occasions that were destroyed during Hurricane Betsy." Betsy had roared through the New Orleans area in 1965, only four years before my wedding, and people were still talking about the destruction it had left in its wake.

As a born worrier, I've always admired my mother-in-law's attitude of living in the present. Over the years I have tried to adapt this philosophy to every facet of life, leading me to believe in the rightness of enjoying the "now" rather than hoarding for the future. I took her advice to heart, and over the years I've set the table with dishes I love, served coffee in my favorite cups, and used the family heirlooms passed down to me by my aunts as often as possible. True, things occasionally get ripped, chipped, or stained, but to me, that just gives them more history.

And I've tried to widen the practice into a way of life. I believe more than ever that time itself is something to be enjoyed today, not hoarded for tomorrow. Today really is the best day to hug your kids or befriend a stranger or tell people just how much they mean to you.

The wisdom of this advice came rushing back to me in August, when Hurricane Katrina hit New Orleans in a way Betsy never did. My mother- and father-in-law lost everything—house, car, beautiful yard, eight decades of possessions. When I first walked into my mother-in-law's home, I was horrified to see dishes, clothing, pictures all piled up in front of her house. But her reaction was true to form—she told me how glad she was that she had enjoyed her possessions when she had them. It reinforced my belief that all we really have power over is today; in a heartbeat, or a hurricane, you can lose it all.

Today they live in an apartment in a strange city an hour out of town, surrounded by household goods that hold no memories. My mother-in-law says she takes great solace in the knowledge that she once served many a family Thanksgiving dinner on her turkey platter, and passed around pounds and pounds of boiled crawfish on the trays now consigned to a dump. We did manage to salvage a few pieces of her crystal from the wreckage, and these she passed out to her daughters-in-law, with a reminder to use and enjoy them. And we do. This Christmas I served guests on a delicately etched glass dish she had received as a wedding present more than sixty years ago. When I pass the platter down to my own daughter-in-law, I'm going to give her the same advice.

Freelance writer JUDI RUSSELL and her husband live in Des Moines, Iowa, after having lived for many years in New Orleans. Ms. Russell enjoys returning to the Big Easy to visit her mother-in-law, who is now a widow.

A Mother's Love

JENNIFER SMITH

I waited several months before meeting my boyfriend Jason's son, Trenton.

What I didn't expect was the quick connection the two of us made. Trenton, the sporty seven-year-old who loves to laugh, and I, the thirty-year-old woman who had always wanted children, became fast friends.

It wasn't until one of Trenton's basketball games that I realized the depth of my love for this boy. As Jason and I sat on the sidelines, we watched the coordinated Trenton run, pass, and shoot the ball fluidly. While he was dribbling the ball down court, Trenton's opponent closely followed.

Somehow Trenton lost control of the ball. It began to roll. He tried to retrieve the ball before it went out of bounds. As Trenton sped up, so did his opponent. Both kids, so focused on the ball, neglected to notice the stage that was quickly approaching in front of them. They picked up speed. I noted the height of the stage and the height of Trenton and saw the potential destruction. Then it happened; Trenton's face collided with the solid wood stage. It made a horrible noise, and he hollered out.

Before I knew it, Jason was over to him and had scooped him up, carrying him like a baby. He held him close and softly consoled him. I wanted to run to them, but I stayed seated. As Jason brought Trenton to our seats, I realized I could hardly see. My eyes were full of tears. My heart was beating hard in my chest. My body wanted to wail for this sweet boy. No serious injury came from his accident, so wailing wasn't necessary. He composed himself quickly, as kids usually do, and returned to the court. As I watched him shake it off, I said to myself, "You're in love with this kid."

I know my reaction to Trenton's accident was a motherly one. The pride I feel when I see him learn new things is something a mother feels. This last year has been hard on our relationship because I've been so consumed with finishing my college degree. I don't always have time to play a game or shoot hoops with him, and he usually understands. But, sometimes, I give in to his sweet, little voice and put my books down.

I did not give birth to Trenton, but I love him as a mother would. I believe that being a mother is more than biology; being a mother is a state of mind. In a recent stress management workshop, I listened to many women express the difficulty in balancing college with motherhood. They talked about the disappointment they saw in their children's eyes, not to mention the disappointment they felt in themselves, for having to turn away their children to study. I found myself shaking my head in agreement. I sympathized with them. And that day, what I'd been feeling with Trenton for nearly two years was clearly defined: I am a mother because I love like one.

After graduating with her bachelor's degree in English from Boise State University, JENNIFER SMITH went on to study for her master's in marriage and family counseling. Although she and Jason parted ways in 2009, the experiences she shared with him and his family helped shape her into the person she is today: the wife of an amazing man, Mike, and the mother of her three-month-old girl, Marlowe Grace.

I Can Make Time

～

LILY LLAMZON DARAIS

My mother was never granted her wish to be a stay-at-home mom, but she made it her priority always to be readily accessible to her children. She was able to negotiate a schedule with her company that allowed her, a corporate lawyer, to be home often by the time her children arrived home from school.

I remember coming home one afternoon after a particularly difficult day in middle school. As soon as my mother saw my tear-stained cheeks, she built a fire in our fireplace, sat down on the couch with me, and stroked my hair for hours while I cried into her lap. Many years later, I have no idea what I was crying about that day, but I remember the security and warmth I felt with my mother's arms around me, knowing that someone was there to focus genuine love and healing attention on my miserable and needy twelve-year-old self.

At the time, I didn't realize what a sacrifice my mother made to spend an afternoon engaged in nothing else but comforting her daughter. Undoubtedly, she spent a late night afterwards cleaning, catching up on the work she'd brought home from the office, and attending to the needs of my father and younger brother. She must have felt harried as she attempted to cram the work of an afternoon into the few short hours she had before midnight, and I suspect she never realized that the lesson she taught me that day would stay with me for as long as it has. That day symbolized, for me, a lesson that she had been teaching me for years—a lesson about love that is palpable, love that considers not only the needs but the desires of the loved, love that gives to the point of sacrifice. It was a small incident, merely representative of a million other such kindnesses, but nevertheless, that afternoon looms large in memory.

Five months ago, I gave birth to a precious daughter who fills my life with purpose and opportunity. Although I give thanks continually for the blessing of being at home full-time with her, I am surprised daily by how hard it is to get simple things done when I have a baby around. My to-do list often faces off with a sweet little girl who wants to be played with and held. I want to give all of my attention to my daughter, but I also want a clean house, family dinners, laundered clothes, and time to maintain other important relationships in my life.

Finding balance is a lot harder than I had anticipated. But whenever I find myself choosing between spending time with my daughter and getting another thing done, I feel the warm love of my mother compelling me onward to give my daughter all that is best in me. As I begin my own journey of motherhood, this I believe: I can make time to listen, stroke hair, share warmth, and sacrifice, all because I have a mother who did that for me.

LILY LLAMZON DARAIS holds an MEd from Harvard and taught reading in the Chicago Public Schools for a year. She is now a stay-at-home mother who lives in Salt Lake City with her husband and daughter.

Our Children

HAYDEH TAKASUGI

He slept cradled in my arms last night, little head on my shoulder, his hand on my chest and his feet tucked into me. I stayed awake listening to his breathing, fascinated by his every move. He giggled in his sleep, and I wondered what could be funny to a one-year-old. I could sense the security he felt; I sensed his body relaxed, his breathing slow and deliberate. The sense of peace that surrounded him was magnificent. A few doors down slept my three-year-old girl, tired by the hustle of her day. I listened to the monitor next to my bed just in case she woke up needing my reassurance that everything was fine, but in these short years she has grown to be an independent child, and those instances are far between.

My home life contrasts starkly with the scene that greets me each morning at work. As a deputy public defender, I see the kids whom society has labeled the worst of the worst—the "gang bangers," the "rapists," the "molesters," the "robbers"—the list goes on. But past those labels, they are still children. As I sit across from them and look into their eyes, I have a chance to talk to them about their lives, their homes, their dreams. I sit through tears, I sit through anger, I sit through indifference, but mostly I sit through hurt. A deep hurt that shines through their eyes. A hurt of being forgotten, abused, abandoned, labeled, and discarded. Some of them come from families who tried to do the very best they could through the limitations of poverty and discrimination. Some come from families who simply didn't care.

I see mothers and fathers, but mostly mothers who sit in the hallways day after day wanting to take their kids home despite the heinous accusations logged against them, to reclaim their children from the vicious streets that have swallowed them whole. I also see mothers and fathers who come to court ready to walk away permanently from their children. And each day at work I see hope abandoned. Each time a child is institutionalized, sent to juvenile prisons, taken to adult court and sentenced to life in prison, our future dreams are relinquished.

I have come to realize that these children are our future, even if we don't want to admit it. They too slept, or yearned to sleep, on a mother's shoulder at night. They too had dreams, hopes, an imagination. But then something happened, something tragic and devastating that robbed them of their youthful joy.

Every day when I go home, I hold my children tightly in my arms and whisper "I love you" over and over again. And yet, even as I am filled with hope for my own kids, I cannot forget those children I leave behind. I live in two worlds, one of promise, one of tragedy. I never forget that these children I work with, no matter what they are accused of, are indeed children. And they are *our* children, and our future.

HAYDEH TAKASUGI is a mother of two and a deputy public defender with the Los Angeles County Public Defender's Office. She spends all of her free time on gym floors and baseball fields.

Being Yourself

CAROLYN WILLIAMSON

My mother has a unique way of embarrassing her children. Whenever she gets excited about something, she jumps up and down, hopping from one foot to another, waving her arms in the air and shrieking in excitement. We call this the "silly dance." As her daughter, I find this completely mortifying. Anytime she goes into the silly dance, my siblings and I will inch slowly away, smile awkwardly, and explain to people, "No, she's not my mother."

Even though my mother embarrassed me to no end when I was a child, and even though she still does the silly dance when something goes her way, I now enjoy it.

The silly dance is who she is, and it shows that she's happy. If she didn't do her dance and just obeyed our wishes of "not in public, Mom," she would be compromising who she is.

My mother dances to her own beat, and many times that beat follows the works of Rogers and Hammerstein, Andrew Lloyd Webber, and the Gershwins. Road trips in my family were always a fun time when we sang songs from *Joseph and the Amazing Technicolor Dreamcoat, Oklahoma,* or *West Side Story*—the musicals that she grew up with.

I owe a lot of my love for the theater to my mother. I now sing show tunes in the shower and in the car. I even sing in public like my mother does, and my friends are always doing that same awkward smile and whispering under their breath, "Carolyn, public."

So in many ways I'm becoming my mother, which for any daughter is a fear of great proportions, but I'm not going to stop singing show tunes just because people feel embarrassed by it—that's not who I am. Although I can't dance very well, when my favorite song comes on the convenience store speaker system, I boogie down the aisles mouthing the words. I have no doubt I will mortify my own children with my rendition of the "silly dance." So what? That's who I am.

I believe everyone should dance to the beat of her own drum, even if the guy next to you gives you a weird look.

If that happens, I pick up a shampoo bottle in aisle seven, use it as a microphone, and continue my jam. I believe in the things that set us apart. I believe in mortifying our children so they will mortify theirs. I believe in being myself, no matter how many awkward smiles I get. I believe in never compromising who I am.

Although she originally wrote her essay as a high school student in Dayton, Ohio, CAROLYN WILLIAMSON is currently a student at the Scripps College of Communication at Ohio University. She continues to write and plans to graduate in 2012 with a degree in communication studies with an emphasis in public advocacy.

We Are Optimists

ANGELA WEST

I believe in a special brand of optimism known only to mothers who have lost babies.

Three years ago, just before Christmas, I had a miscarriage. Everyone said what people always say at such a time. Miscarriage is common. It's nature's way of preventing birth defects. How lucky we were that it was so early. How lucky we were to already have a child. Next time everything would be fine. I went on to lose two more babies the following year. Everything definitely wasn't fine. I wasn't fine.

A year after our first loss, I attended my first Empty Arms meeting. It took all my courage, and my husband's support, for me to go. I was afraid that no one would be there. I was afraid that my losses somehow weren't awful enough to entitle me to mourn with women who had lost older babies, babies the world viewed as somehow more real. I found a group of people who were more supportive and understanding than I could have ever imagined.

There were women there who had lost babies to premature labor, horrible birth defects, and genetic diseases; women who lost full-term babies to such things as cord accidents and SIDS; and women like me who lost babies before they even had a chance to feel them move. They are some of the bravest women I have ever known. They helped me survive my grief. They helped me survive the overwhelming fear I suffered throughout my fifth pregnancy, which resulted in my beautiful, healthy baby girl. And they helped me realize something.

We are optimists. Most people would not think of us that way. On the surface, we do not appear optimistic. We ache for those we've lost. We cry in our cars and in our showers. We panic through our pregnancies. We dread sonograms and baby showers. We drive doctors crazy with requests to hear heartbeats. We check our babies' breathing innumerable times. We fear our children's every cold; we blow every bump, bruise, or strange symptom out of all proportion. We even check our husbands' breathing in the middle of the night. But we are optimists.

We face the panic and move on. We struggle through tests, fertility treatments, foster programs, and fear to have our babies. We try and try again. We dream and pray and fight and believe. We risk repeated loss, repeated failure, repeated pain for ourselves and our dearest ones. We believe that our babies still are.

We are survivors of infant loss. We grieve always, we fear always, and yet still we love. I believe we are optimists.

ANGELA WEST lives in Lake City, Pennsylvania, with her husband, Chris, and her two living children, Ethan and Elanor. She works at a print shop, and hopes to someday write a guide to surviving miscarriage. She still attends Empty Arms meetings on a regular basis.

Hope Dished Out in Plenty

DAVID E. COWEN

I believe in Mama's Sunshine Salad.

Sunshine Salad was my mother's recipe for a mixture of orange gelatin, shredded carrots, and chunks of pineapple with its juice substituted for one cup of the water. It's a recipe common to many families, but special to mine. This concoction and its simple ingredients exemplified how Mama always said she lived her life: "I did the best I could with what I had." Mama often joked that although she had been born in Prosperity, Missouri, she had lived in poverty all her life.

My first memory of Mama serving Sunshine Salad was Thanksgiving, 1964. That past year, my father died of cancer, leaving Mama with eleven children. The same week he died, our house was consumed in a fire. Despite living through the darkest time of my life, where hope seemed to be a luxury for those more favored, Mama saved her money to make sure this first Thanksgiving meal was something special. I remember eating that scoop of orange salad with its cold, tangy sweetness. Because it was cheap to make, my siblings and I could eat as much as we wanted. It was pure joy. It was hope dished out in plenty.

Mama served it every Thanksgiving thereafter. As my siblings and I struggled to overcome this lean existence, Mama's Sunshine Salad was one of those constants that always bound us. We took for granted it would always be there, like Mama. Some years, Mama would suggest she try a different dish, something more creative. But at least one of us would beg, and she would give in. It was a symbol of the foundation of our family—of knowing that in our family, we could find the hope to carry on.

To feed us Mama worked up to three jobs at a time. She even went back to college at age fifty-one to work on her master's and PhD in English. After graduating, my mother went back to our hometown to teach college, a lifelong dream fulfilled. For us, she had always been the ultimate teacher.

Most of us put ourselves through college and gradu-ate schools. We individually worked to become success-ful in business, teaching, and law. We introduced Mama's

Sunshine Salad to our children and made it a staple of our families. It is one of the things they can count on now: a constant reassurance of hope, love, and faith in family, and a remembrance of Mama's struggles to overcome.

Last year, Mama passed away a week before Thanksgiving at the age of ninety-one. We all agreed to honor her by celebrating Thanksgiving dinner the day after her funeral. Of course we served Sunshine Salad. We smiled as that orange joy soothed our throats. She may be gone, but we can still taste her love every Thanksgiving.

It is not a gourmet dish, but it keeps her part of what we are. That is why I believe in Mama's Sunshine Salad.

DAVID E. COWEN, the tenth child of his mother, Virginia Cowen, lives in Houston, Texas, with his wife and two sons, and practices law in Galveston, Texas. He has published a volume of poetry about his childhood in Brownsville, Texas. Mr. Cowen and his wife make their own version of Sunshine Salad every Thanksgiving.

Saviors

LISA HOLMES

My mother buries flies. The ones that make it to greet the approach of winter and then end up dead in the corners of windowsills. I've never seen her do it, but I imagine her careful hands. Her quiet. There is something my mother understands about the fly's last breath, its struggle against the cold, its futile attempt to outlive winter. My mother has lived through the unimaginable loss of a child. She has survived breast cancer. And she buries flies because she believes that no one's struggle, not even that of the smallest sort of someone, should go unnoticed.

One of my best memories of growing up is snuggling with my mother in bed watching *Little House on the Prairie.* Sharing the same pillow, her arm around me. There simply wasn't a safer place for me to be. And I remember her face, many years later, after the first of a few breakups with my high school boyfriend, a little sad and a little angry. And I understood, even then, that she wanted to save me from the world—from growing up and losing the things and people I loved, from pain in general. And she knew she couldn't. After the final breakup with this same boyfriend, it was my mother who drove a thousand miles to help me pack up my things and move on (both literally and figuratively), because I wasn't able to pull it together and do it on my own. This care that my mother offered me when I was growing up created the roots of my own ability to sympathize and empathize.

Long before I discovered my mother's fly burial grounds, I was conducting my own rituals intended to ease the lives of these small beings. My friend Jenny and I used to rescue flies from little-boy prisons of knot-tied thread. How those boys were able to tie thread around such tiny bodies so that they could still fly, leashed, in circles, is something I never knew or have since forgotten. But I do remember collecting them at the end of the day, taking them home, putting them in slide-out matchboxes lined with tissues—a regular fly hospital. None of them were nursed back to health. All of them died despite our attentive care. I hated those boys.

You could say it's about the helplessness of the fly—that I rescued them, and my mother buries them, simply because we feel sorry for them. But if you said that, you'd miss the finer point, which is that I have learned from my mother that compassion has a place in this world. I believe that nothing and no one is inconsequential. I believe that every little thing deserves a fair chance, that all struggle screams out for some kind of notice, and that although we probably can't save anyone from pain and loss, we should doggone well try.

LISA HOLMES has been teaching for the last twenty years, and she currently mentors teenagers who go to school online. She is an urban homesteader who enjoys gardening, baking, seeing live music, and meeting new people. She lives in Boulder, Colorado, with her husband and daughter, dogs, fish, and chickens.

Raising Kane

∿

SHANNON BLADY

I've been raising my son, Kane, since I was seventeen years old. My life has revolved around him since that cold Christmas Eve when he came home from the hospital.

I discovered that I was pregnant in my junior year at a rigorous honors high school. Saying "Congratulations" to a woman who announces she's pregnant still feels foreign to me. My aunts, parents, grandparents all shared that same dejected look, as if bidding farewell to a close friend. No diplomas hung in any of their homes then, and all their hopes were pinned on me. When they found out I was pregnant, they figured I could probably finish high school, but no one even discussed college at that point. They thought my future had just taken a turn for the worse.

I ended up receiving a complete educational scholarship to our local university and raised my son on campus between classes. I had no bills then, no plans. I just wanted to be a college graduate, be a good mom, and make a difference in the world. My college years were spent enjoying my son's milestones and adjusting to the chasm that had grown between his father and me.

Kane cried for his bottle at my high school graduation and played patiently with his Matchbox cars at my college graduation four years later. Raising him inspired me to become a teacher. I thought I had accomplished it all, setting straight those looks of dismay and not becoming another statistic. But now he's twelve, and his mother is unmarried and often mistaken for his older sister.

When administrators, colleagues, or parents of my students discover that I have a son, I get the familiar question, "How old is he?" And when I answer them, I see their entire perception of me change. Then I can mouth in sync with them, "You don't look old enough to have a child that age." They want me to tell them exactly how old I am. It's as if they want to know how someone could let that happen, how it's possible for someone like me, a professional, to have had a storied past. I just answer, "Well, I am. And he's phenomenal."

It has been tough at times, but I have relied on my family and a handful of true friends. It's also complicated to justify my past to a boy who is coming of age. But as he grows older, I realize that he's become a caring, conscientious person, and I know that I had something to do with that.

Of course I don't advocate teen pregnancy, but I've been on a beautiful ride since giving birth to Kane. I believe that a teenage mother is still a mother. I am not a statistic. I am not a burden to society. Being a teenage mother did not force me to quit school—or anything, ever. Because I did it. I'm still doing it. I will always be raising Kane.

SHANNON BLADY is an educator in San Antonio, Texas. She is currently pursuing a PhD in interdisciplinary learning and teaching at the University of Texas at San Antonio. Her son, Kane, is now a freshman at the same university.

Mom's Everyday Advice

LEA CASSEL MATTHEWS

One of my mom's favorite things to say is, "Do the right thing, at the right time, and you will never be sorry." While I was growing up, those words didn't mean very much to me. I would just wrinkle my nose and groan every time I heard them.

This year, with the thought of going away to college rising in my consciousness, I have found myself reflecting on that advice. I believe the quality of our life is defined when doing the right thing transcends from us to benefit someone else. It isn't found in those extraordinary moments of pivotal resolve, but rather in everyday, more ordinary times, when we have the opportunity to brighten someone's day or make someone smile. The deeds that really make a difference in our lives are the simple acts that don't take much effort, like a quick phone call to thank someone for a kindness or to see how a friend is feeling if he or she hasn't been well.

When my grandfather was sick, I heard Mom saying, "Call right now." I had just gotten home from school, and all I wanted to do was relax, but I made the call. After hearing the gratitude in my grandfather's voice and knowing how much it meant to him, I knew I "did the right thing at the right time."

When my cousin asked me to help her put a scrapbook together for our grandmother's eightieth birthday, I heard Mom say, "Do the right thing at the right time." Each time my cousin called, I had something more important to do first. My cousin put the scrapbook together by herself, and I will never forget how small I felt when she presented it to Gram and said it was from both of us.

"Doing the right thing at the right time" is paramount. It speaks to our integrity and the very core essence of who we are. Anything can be said by words, but actions prove our level of commitment to our ideals and values. They're the testament of what we profess to be true.

I'm not sure what college I will be attending next year, but I am sure that Mom's words will be echoing around me.

When the lonely girl in the dorm room across the hall is by herself, I will hear Mom say, "Do the right thing," and I will invite her to dinner. When a friend needs help studying for a final exam, I will hear Mom say, "at the right time," and I will help her when she asks. When I see a friend hurting herself with an eating disorder, I will hear Mom say, "You will never be sorry," and I will take her to a doctor. Those words that I didn't think about much growing up have become a part of me, without my even realizing it. My commitment will always be to "do the right thing, at the right time," so I will never be sorry.

LEA CASSEL MATTHEWS is a native of Murrysville, Pennsylvania (a suburb of Pittsburgh). Ms. Matthews currently attends Duquesne University and plans to become the fifth-generation dentist in her family. She had the opportunity to spend two summers studying dance in Italy and has recently signed on with the e-magazine *Sweet Lemon* as a contributing author.

Mother and Me

JAMIE LEMKE-BARRAND

I believe in second chances.

I can remember with great clarity an evening when I was three or four years old, standing in my sleeveless, Winnie-the-Pooh patterned nightgown on the front porch of my home in New Jersey, pounding on the door to be let in.

It was dusk. My mother had locked me out.

I don't remember exactly why. I was probably being naughty and she'd had enough of me.

I've always been naughty. My mother will tell you that. I was a naughty child, an out-of-control teenager, and now I am a hopeless adult who lies and screws things up left and right.

She's right. I do screw things up and then lie about it. I am so terrified of my mother's disapproval—so scared of not being loved—that I will say anything to hold on to her.

I know myself well enough to know that I'm an impulsive, irrational woman who does things without thinking. I have always been that way; anyone who knows me will tell you that. My mother has been trying to change me for as long as I can remember, mold me into the image of her and my twin sister, who is a carbon copy of our mother: responsible, honest, good, moral, upstanding.

I am none of those things, at least not to the degree that they are. I never have been. I never will be.

I know my mother loves me, but I also know it's because she has to. She doesn't like me. If we were not related, I am not the sort of person my mother would be friends with. No, she would not.

As I have grown older, I have come to understand that people are who and what they are. She is. I am. And we are far too different to be friends. She has tried to help me, and I love her for that.

Now I am in my own house. I will never have to be on the porch again, because in my house, I am loved and accepted. I mess up, and I am met with loving arms assuring me that there is nothing that can't be fixed there.

My children will never be on the porch. I have promised this to them and to myself. They will buck my authority.

They will break my things and my heart. They will be naughty. But they will never, ever have to pound on the door to be let in.

JAMIE LEMKE-BARRAND is married, has two children, and lives in central Indiana. She has worked as a newspaper reporter since 1995 and has won many awards for her reporting. She currently works for a small daily newspaper in Crawfordsville, Indiana. Her essay was written several years ago, and with much love, effort, and patience on both sides, Ms. Lemke-Barrand and her mother have since reconciled.

Considering Adoption

SUSIE M. GREEN

My vision of having more children did not die when I divorced. I, along with my two birth children, ages eleven and six, lived in a public housing project in Washington, DC.

The idea to adopt a child came to the forefront of my mind when I heard a civic announcement in church, which described the concept of "one church, one child." If a member of each church were to adopt one child, the number of foster children would be significantly reduced.

I knew I had enough love to give, so without considering that I had no extra bedroom and that my income was barely enough to sustain us, I applied to adopt a toddler.

Two-year-old Henry had a sporadic rocking problem. During waking hours he rocked on his knees, and then at night he rocked in his bed so violently that I had to tie the post of his bed to my bed to keep him from rocking his crib across the room. The social worker had not mentioned this. Maybe she did not know, because Henry had lived in a homeless shelter and two foster homes. But now he was mine, and with him came his rocking.

To calm his rocking, I bought a rocking chair. I rocked him every day as I sang happy songs. The harder he rocked on my lap, the louder I sang. After months of rocking, one day the rocking chair collapsed and we both fell flat on the floor! Shocked at suddenly finding ourselves on the floor, I began to laugh—and then he laughed. We sat there laughing for a while. With him still in my arms, I stood up, assessed the damage, and together we carried the chair, piece by piece, out to the alley for the trash truck.

Years passed, yet Henry's rocking did not stop. My patience was tried both at home and in public when he rocked, but my capacity to become more patient grew beyond belief. My concern for why he rocked and how I could soothe him grew despite his missing family history. The more he grew physically, the more I grew spiritually and emotionally. But I had three children—not just one—and there was no time to be obsessed about finding out his history, although something inside me always wonders what his birth parents were like.

This I believe: for many people it is not the unknown about an adoptive child that is most feared. Rather it is what we do not know about ourselves that stops us dead in our tracks when considering adoption. We do not fear whether the child will love us, but whether we have the capacity to understand and to love the child. The most profound lesson I learned was about me. I became determined to accept what I discovered, to understand what I learned, and to love all I knew.

Today Henry is a junior in college, a member of the U.S. Air Force National Guard, and a Department of Defense IT contractor working in northern Virginia. He is healthy and happy, and rocking only to his favorite music.

SUSIE M. (HARRIS) GREEN enjoyed a career as a senior computer specialist with the Federal Deposit Insurance Corporation. Following her retirement, she studied psychology and African American history at George Mason University and Oxford University, and earned a BA degree from Bluefield State College. Ms. Green has three children, is fond of gardening and travel, and cherishes time with her grandchildren. She currently resides in southwest Virginia.

The Eternal Sunshine

TRACI HIGGINS

When I was seven, I used to go door-to-door with my mother in the housing project where I grew up. She knocked on doors and asked the residents for donations to the American Lung Association. Some would give a few coins; others, on rare occasions, a whole dollar; but most would silently shake their heads "No." No matter the amount, my mother thanked the giver; wrote his or her name, address, and offerings on her large, white-lined envelope; and placed the money inside.

After what seemed an eternity, though actually just a few hours, we returned to our apartment, and my mother counted the money. The yield didn't match the effort: I don't think she collected more than $10. Still, she sent the skimpy collection to the organization whose logo was on the front. I remember thinking it looked like a red telephone pole.

Even as a child, I knew my mother's actions were extraordinary. Asking poor people to give to an organization whose mission held no perceptible connection to their daily struggles to put food on the table, clothes on their children, and a roof over their head wasn't what you did. Other charities gave to these folks; you didn't ask them to give. To them, her efforts likely seemed foolish.

Fortunately for me, my mother followed her own beat. She'd regularly sweep up trash on the sidewalk, shovel the common walkway after a snow, and plant flowers year after year—marigolds and petunias—to complement the gloriously perennial purple irises that ringed our small front garden.

Although my charitable giving is modest, I faithfully and regularly donate to causes to fight AIDS; to stop genocide, hunger, and homelessness; to support public broadcasting, the arts, and public education; and to heal families. And I volunteer my time to empower little girls and fix our badly broken public schools.

I do these things because I believe I've been given much, so much is required of me. The me who trudged along with my mother on a seeming fool's errand knows that the why of it took shape long before I could explain my motivations. I never asked my mother why she collected those donations, and, ironically, the lung cancer that killed her twenty-one years ago prevents me from asking now.

But had I asked, my mother's response would've been simple: "because I can." That's what she would've said. But from that *look* in her eyes and her daily efforts to make life a bit brighter, I know she also acted on hope—hope that tomorrow would be better, hope that her actions somehow would make a difference, and hope that the peace she felt giving herself over to these possibilities would sustain and carry her forward to see the sunshine of another day.

A former Peace Corps volunteer, TRACI HIGGINS has served as counsel to the 1999 FIFA Women's World Cup and PBS, and has advanced education reform for Washington, DC, public schools. She lives in DC, where she continues to honor her mother's lessons and is general counsel at the Thelonious Monk Institute of Jazz.

Don't Tell Me How Rocky the Sea Is—Just Bring in the Ship

CHRISTINE JARVIS

One night in fall 2007, after being newly diagnosed with Alzheimer's disease, my mother sat with me on her bed, both of us crying. The words "nursing home" were never said, but were clearly on Mom's mind.

"All I want is to stay here with you," Mom told me. "But whatever you have to do, I will understand."

My mother was from Friesland in the Netherlands and lived her life by the Dutch motto, "Don't tell me how rocky the sea is—just bring in the ship."

"No nursing home—not now, not ever," I said to myself that night.

When it was no longer safe for Mom to be alone, I hired a caregiver to stay with her while I was at work. I took the other shifts: four o'clock until next morning, weekends, holidays. Daughter/caregiver 24/7.

One day, Mom said, "Why do you call me Mom? I *like* it, but why do you do that?"

I answered, "Because you *are* my mother."

The look on her face told me she didn't believe me; she no longer knew who I was. It didn't matter—I knew.

All too quickly, we went through the stages of the disease: complete memory loss, aggression, fear that grew to paranoia, loss of speech, sleepless nights, and a physical deterioration that soon saw Mom bedbound and incontinent. Pressure sores, loss of appetite, and an inability to swallow even liquids soon followed.

Caregivers tell each other to "never let them see you cry." Horsefeathers! I was losing my mother. Why shouldn't I cry? I was sad beyond measure; why shouldn't my mother know that?

I slept more often in Mom's bed than in my own room. Mom often drifted off to sleep stroking my arm or patting me gently on the shoulder. She didn't know who I was, but she could recognize sadness when she saw it, and still, in her motherly role, she offered what comfort she could.

Finally, knowing the end could be only weeks away, I took compassionate leave from work. My leave started on September 14, a Tuesday. A friend came to stay overnight, determined to support me in supporting my mother. My friend took first watch that first night. In the early hours of Wednesday, my friend woke me and said, "Your mother's breathing has changed. I think you should come."

I went to Mom's room, crawled into the bed beside her, and held her. I couldn't believe she was dying—not on the first day of my being home with her. It wasn't supposed to be that soon. Within minutes, though, Mom was gone.

Most of us won't do great things in life, but I believe in doing the small things we are called upon to do. Rocky sea or calm, we can bring in the ship with grace and courage. I couldn't stop Mom's Alzheimer's journey once it started, but I could make the journey with her. I couldn't hold back the inevitable, but I could hold my mother in my arms when she reached her journey's end.

On September 15, 2010, at the age of eighty-four, Jannie Jarvis died peacefully in her own bed in her own home, in her daughter's arms. Calm seas and safe harbor, Mom.

CHRISTINE JARVIS was born and lives in Toronto, Canada. She is a contributing writer at Suite101.com, and she writes a blog called Once a Caregiver. Ms. Jarvis's interests include reading mysteries and mainstream and historical fiction, social justice, human dignity, strong women, aging with challenges, and lifelong learning. She lists being Jannie's daughter and Nancy's friend among her achievements.

Simple Saturdays

STEFANIE WASS

Are you signing up your kids for something?"

My friend is thumbing through the local community education catalogue, marking important class dates with a ballpoint pen.

"Definitely swimming lessons," she says, completing the class registration form.

"When are they going?" I ask, thinking of my own two girls, not yet proficient at the front crawl or backstroke.

"Saturday mornings."

"Oh," I hesitate. "We don't really do much on Saturdays."

"It's not too bad," she assures me. "It doesn't start until ten."

I picture myself at 10 AM on Saturday, still in my pink pajamas, sipping a second cup of hazelnut coffee. My girls, clad in princess pj's and fuzzy monkey slippers, are busy hosting a doll tea party. My husband, outstretched on the sofa, is lost in a biography. Our kitchen holds the evidence of an earlier feast: sticky maple syrup decorates the tablecloth, and a box of pancake mix sits aside the electric griddle. The dishes, stacked high in the sink, will have to wait. I have a newspaper to read, a magazine to peruse. It is Saturday morning: a well-earned day of laziness in a harried world.

My Saturdays haven't always been simple. When I was a young girl, each Saturday began with ice skating lessons, followed by a half-hour drive to a downtown Cleveland music conservatory for piano and violin instruction. Mom was my chauffeur, pulling over at the McDonald's drive-through to buy burgers and shakes, which we ate en route. Despite this schedule, I loved every minute of my Saturdays with Mom. Because she worked full-time as a second-shift industrial nurse, I didn't see her nearly enough during the week. Even today, she recalls our Saturday mornings with fondness. "Remember how we'd drive to the Institute?" she says. "And then get something to eat?"

Thirty years later, I am a mother. My weekdays are filled with novel writing, volunteering, and driving my girls to and from Girl Scouts, music lessons, and church activities. By week's end, I yearn for a lazy day. Perhaps it is selfish, but I like to turn off the alarm clock and dream about hotcakes and bacon. At our house, Saturdays are about simplicity: no errands, lessons, or sports practices.

I believe that simple Saturdays are good for my daughters. Laughter fills the house as we spend relaxed time together as a family.

"Can I crack the eggs for the pancakes, Daddy?" my youngest asks, twirling around the kitchen, a spatula in one hand.

"Mama, you slept in again!" teases my eldest as I stumble into the kitchen, rubbing my eyes as I search for my coffee mug.

I know my girls are watching, and I hope they remember: everyone needs a day to recharge and reconnect. Saturday is sacred: a lazy day full of promise, a gift to spend as we please.

STEFANIE WASS's stories have been published in the *Los Angeles Times, Seattle Times, Christian Science Monitor, Akron Beacon Journal, Akron Life and Leisure, Cleveland Magazine,* and *The Writer,* as well as three *Cup of Comfort* and ten *Chicken Soup for the Soul* books. She hopes to publish her novel for middle school readers. Please visit www .stefaniewass.com.

Memories of Lessons Learned

MARY LOU HURLEY

I believe in the power of example. When my first child was born sixteen years ago, my mother did not visit me in the hospital or stay with me for a week. She had died twenty years earlier, when I was fourteen. I could not call her when my son was colicky or wouldn't take a bottle. Instead, I called on memories of her when I was growing up. My memories of her are how I learned to be a mother.

When my son cried in the middle of the night, I wondered if I should pick him up or let him cry. I wracked my brain, but could not think of a time when my mother did not comfort me as a child. So I picked him up.

I create alone time with each of my kids: a girls' night at the movies or shopping with my daughter, watching ESPN or taking a walk with my son. "This is nice," I say. "Just the two of us." My mother and I ate the best hot dog I ever had at the counter in Kresge's department store in downtown Bloomfield, New Jersey. My three brothers were left behind with my father.

"This is nice," my mother said. "Just the two of us."

"Yeah," I sighed. "No boys."

From her, I learned to cherish the fact that my kids aren't like me. I love that my daughter is outspoken and thinks outside the box, nearly the opposite of me at her age. I was a shy tomboy who loved baseball, climbing trees, and riding my bike fast enough to leave skid marks when I hit the brakes. My mother was articulate and ladylike and had no interest in sports. When I asked her why she didn't accompany us on our annual journey to Yankee Stadium, she said, "It's boring. I used to read a book when I went with your father."

"You read a book at Yankee Stadium?" I asked with the righteous indignation of a seven-year-old.

She smiled and packed our lunches and jackets for Opening Day, and feigned interest in the game when we returned. She encouraged my love of sports, let me run wild in the neighborhood, and never told me to act like a lady.

When she was dying, she lived in the moment. "I'm only going to die once," she said. "There's no point putting myself through it over and over again in my mind." Her face bloated, her hair prematurely gray, she attended my brother's eighth-grade graduation in a wheelchair and threw a party for him that night. She died two weeks later.

Her example taught me not to fear death or any scary challenge in my life, including a job loss or my father's failing health last year. I try not to put myself through such experiences until they actually happen. Like my mother, I want to live in the moment and be grateful for what I have in the present.

I hope to pass that lesson along to my kids, too.

MARY LOU HURLEY is a medical writer and editor. She lives in northern New Jersey with her husband and two children, who have very different personalities but are both avid fans of the New York Yankees.

A Parent at Home

LISA CRYSTAL

I was a quasi-latchkey child. The daughter of a single working mom, I'd walk home from school each day and carefully unlock our apartment door, lingering in the silent living room as I dropped off my books. Then, with grim resignation, I trudged to the neighbors' apartment to watch TV on their shag carpet while I waited for my mom to get home. On paper, it looked good: the neighbor kids were about my age, and their mom served junk food. But in truth, I hated it. I longed for snacks prepared by my own mom, toys from my own room, TV shows that seemed funnier when viewed from my own shag carpet.

Summer wasn't much better. I was packed off to day camp, and the days were a blur of Popsicle-stick crafts, kickball games played in stifling heat, and lunches of lukewarm sandwiches and milk. Oh, how I yearned for home! I wanted to eat breakfast in my pajamas, climb the oak tree across the street, rearrange my dollhouse furniture.

I knew my mom had no choice. For her, it was work or welfare. But growing up, I vowed to someday become a stay-at-home parent myself. When my oldest was a baby, I chose to spend an extra year at my job to finance our first home purchase. But for the past eighteen years, my husband's salary, careful budgeting, and my part-time freelance income have kept us afloat—and me at home. There have been sacrifices: restaurant dining and vacations are rare events, and my husband has been laid off several times, prompting us to question my decision to forgo a full-time position with health benefits.

But I believe the less tangible benefits have been worth the worry and the sacrifice. After school, I greet my children with hugs and treats. I drive them to sports or scouts, or simply listen as they recount their day. My children do homework in their rooms, rather than on the gym bleachers of the after-school program. During summer, they practice magic tricks and build Lego structures in our living room. They learned to swim in a shallow pool we assembled in our backyard.

In summer, the kids enjoy an occasional art class at our community center, which also operates a day camp for children of working parents. One afternoon I noticed a little girl lagging at the rear of the camp snack line as she studied the wall clock. She reminded me of the girl I once was, counting the minutes until my mom arrived. I smiled at her encouragingly, hoping her cherry Popsicle would help the time pass more quickly.

Eating Popsicles at home with my own children, I am grateful to be here, and I believe my children are too. For here, in the shade of our backyard tree, I do believe a summertime treat tastes that much sweeter.

LISA CRYSTAL is a part-time freelance writer and editor who works from her home in northern California. She is the mother of a daughter and twin sons, all homeschooled at various times, and all of whom say they hope to spend lots of time at home with their own kids someday.

Expect to Have Enough

JODI ACKERMAN FRANK

Expect the unexpected. As parents we must continually remind ourselves of that lesson, even as we teach it to our children.

Expecting something that in the end is not so can be a painful pill to swallow. The opposite is true, too. For instance, thinking of the stories so many women shared, I thought I'd be sick for the first three months of my recent pregnancy and be a bloated, miserable wreck for the rest. In fact, during the first six months, I never felt healthier. Labor, however, was a different story. My Lamaze instructor warned me, "No matter how hard you try, you cannot plan your labor."

I tried anyway.

I wanted to go the natural birth route; I didn't think I'd actually need pain medication unless absolutely necessary. Although I knew the average labor period for a first-time mother was twenty-four hours, I thought mine might be half as long, given my excellent health and exercise routine.

As it turned out, my labor lasted thirty hours. For three days, I was connected to an IV administering Pitocin to induce me, plus pain medication and antibiotics.

When I finally gave birth to Sage Alissa I didn't know what to expect of my daughter or myself. I wanted to marvel at this completely separate human being that just unfolded like a blossom out of my body. But I was too exhausted.

I was also afraid. I had never changed a diaper in my whole thirty-six years. And, growing up with an alcoholic mother and no father, I had no immediate role model to follow. Sure, I could give you the intellectual spiel on how to raise a child, according to the experts. But, frankly, I didn't know where to start. So my husband began by asking the nurse to show him how to change a diaper. In turn, he taught me.

I still don't know what to expect. When will she start walking? When will she get her first tooth? When will she start saying, "No!"? And then there is the bigger picture. What will her life be like five, ten, even thirty years from now? How will she cope in a world of poverty and violence, of injustices and excessive materialism?

My little girl is seven months now. When she looks at me, she really looks, drinking me in for long moments with her daddy's china-blue eyes. One day, she is going to look at me and expect all the answers. I, no doubt, will instead add to her questions.

I feel helpless sometimes knowing that I can't give her everything she wants or needs. What I can give her are some insights into day-to-day living: use only what you need, don't litter, make peace with the next-door neighbor, and try to make a difference in all the other small ways a single person can.

I can offer her my belief that if you work hard and keep asking questions until you are satisfied, you may not get everything you expect, but you'll have enough and you'll be happy. This I believe.

JODI ACKERMAN FRANK is a freelance writer and editor in Saratoga Springs, New York. She enjoys spending time with her daughter and husband, seeking out unexpected surprises on mountain trails and other outdoor adventures.

The Transformative Power
of Letting Go

MARY LACY PORTER

I believe in the transformative power of letting go. I believe that relinquishing expectations about how life is "supposed" to unfold has opened my heart to a more authentic me and a world of infinite possibilities.

My oldest daughter has been a particularly effective teacher of this fundamental truth, although at times her methods have been particularly harsh. The joy of parenting a bright, creative, and energetic child devolved into a nightmare. During her adolescence, I struggled to deal with her combative behavior, substance abuse, run-ins with the law, dropping out of school, and two heartbreaking suicide attempts. Although I brought to bear every imaginable resource in an effort to support, guide, and protect her, I came to realize that the journey she had chosen was hers and hers alone.

Of course I wanted, as all parents do, for my child to be healthy and happy. But I also admit that I wanted her to conform to certain norms simply because it would be more comfortable for me. I would have preferred not to experience the awkward change of subject when I entered a room where parents were discussing their child's college plans, or to endure the curiosity of neighbors wondering why police cars were once again in front of our home. Eventually, however, I came to see my challenge as embracing the uncertainty of what my daughter's process to wholeness was going to look like. To help her grow, I had to let go of where I thought she should be and how I thought she should get there. Choosing to focus on who I knew her to be underneath all that debris helped me let go of the notion that I should (or could) dictate how her life would unfold.

After a number of turbulent years, my daughter has reconnected with her soulful nature and has rediscovered her playful spirit. She thanks me for never giving up on her. She says there is no one else who she would want to be her mom. I now experience the unequaled joy of having a daughter whom I genuinely admire and whose friendship I treasure.

Letting go of trying to govern my daughter's journey has become the catalyst for me to reexamine my own life's path. I realized that my self-imposed expectations about what I *should* be doing to maintain the lifestyle I *ought* to have stood between me and a more authentic life. I recently moved to a less expensive house and left my job as an attorney at a big corporate law firm. It had become too painful to go to work every day and feel so disconnected from my true self. I find myself in unfamiliar, uncomfortable territory, having let go of safety and certainty for the promise of the unknown. Right now, the anxiety of abandoning a career that has defined me for over twenty years threatens to overwhelm me. But I have come to believe that pursuing an enriching life requires a willingness to abandon solid ground, trusting that the wisdom of the heart, if given the chance, will show the way. This is the gift I gave my daughter. This is the gift I am learning to give myself.

MARY LACY PORTER is currently writing a memoir exploring her experiences as a mother and her spiritual path to joy and wholeness. She lives in Baltimore with her husband, and is continually inspired and awed by her two daughters, now in college.

My Mother Is Beautiful

KELSEY MORGAN

My entire life, I have been reminded that my parents are different from those of my friends. They are often mistaken for my grandparents, which always embarrassed me. I was born in 1991, when my mother was forty-five and my father was forty-nine. I guess it was a shock to most people that my mother was pregnant at that age, and I've always feared that I was the "accident" child—the daughter nobody wanted.

During summer vacation when I was ten years old, I began looking through old pictures of my family while my mother was away at work. I found many photos of a beautiful blonde woman. She was the most attractive person I had ever seen. I brought them to my dad to ask who she was.

"That's your mother," he said. "Wasn't she beautiful?"

She absolutely was. I set out to find as many pictures of her as I could. I gazed at them for hours, dreaming of the day when I would look just like her: porcelain skin, bright blue eyes, the most infectious smile, and a striking shade of gorgeous blonde hair. I spent many summers thereafter going through these pictures, finding new ones all the time, and putting them neatly away before my mother got home. It wasn't until I was older that I saw the beauty inside my mother.

Two years ago, a cousin I hardly knew passed away in her sleep. I reluctantly went to the funeral with my parents and spent most of the time sitting with my father while my mom comforted her brother and sister-in-law. My grieving aunt was sobbing and shaking with sadness, her hand holding a tissue under her nose, her eyes fixed on her deceased daughter. My mother took my aunt's free hand in hers and held it for the rest of the viewing. I had never been more proud of my mother than at that moment, and I have never thought her to be more beautiful. I hadn't seen before how much I took her beauty and kindness for granted. I've never been embarrassed of her since.

Growing up, all I cared about was how pretty I could make myself, whether it was in dance costumes, for

Halloween, or just going to school. But my mother taught me the importance of being beautiful from the inside out, rather than the outside in. She showed me that beauty comes from the heart, and our actions are an outward reflection of that beauty.

Today, I am a twenty-year-old college student. My mother is sixty-five, and she is still the most beautiful woman I have ever encountered. She is my best friend. Sometimes she comments about how unattractive she is, but I wouldn't want her any other way. I still dream of one day looking just like my mother, and of having the same strength, kindness, and love that she does. I believe that someday I will.

KELSEY MORGAN is studying sociology at Bowling Green State University in Ohio. She has a passion for creating opportunities for at-risk children who live in urban environments. She currently lives with her parents in Waynesburg, Pennsylvania.

The Gift

KERI FREEBURG

As my child began to grow and move inside me, I sensed her presence, and considered that I had nothing to give her apart from my love. I wondered, "Would that be enough?" I knew that she deserved more: two parents—a mother and a father, a loving couple—who would love her and who were prepared to give her a life with stability and promise.

When I learned of a young couple in their late twenties who were desperately seeking to adopt a newborn baby, I thought this might be the perfect arrangement. Although the adoption would be closed and I would not be able to meet the prospective parents, they came highly recommended, and I quickly gave my consent.

My daughter was born just six days before Christmas at Methodist Hospital, the same hospital where I had been born eighteen years earlier. I was discouraged from seeing her by the nurses and hospital staff, but I do remember catching a glimpse of her before the nurses took her away. Only three days after her birth, I knew that the happy young couple was just down the hall, anxiously waiting to take their newborn daughter home. As I was being discharged from the hospital, I signed the final release. Unable to hold back my tears, I sat on the edge of the hospital bed and prayed that I had made the right choice.

Over the years, my baby girl stayed in my thoughts, especially on her birthday and Christmas. I wondered if she knew about me and whether she would one day find me.

Many years later, in August of 2003, I was thrilled to receive a letter from her. As I looked through the enclosed photographs, I asked God, "Is this really my daughter?" Her name was Melissa, and she was beautiful! My heart was overwhelmed at the sight of her big brown eyes and beautiful smile. Tears flowed down my cheeks as I read the sweet words she had written to me:

"I have always known that I was adopted, ever since I can remember, and I have always thought that I would want to search for you someday so that I could thank you for my life. I was adopted by wonderful parents that I believe were chosen especially for me by God. I was even born on my mother's birthday! I have had a truly blessed life."

In that moment I knew with no uncertainty that I had made the right choice in giving Melissa to that young couple twenty-eight years earlier, and in return they had given her everything that I could not. God's gift to me now is knowing her and being a part of her life. I believe in giving.

KERI FREEBURG has lived on Kodiak Island, Alaska, with her husband, Charlie, the love of her life, for the better part of twenty years. Ms. Freeburg is originally from Texas, where she was reunited with her daughter, Melissa, in 2003. Although they are separated by several thousand miles, they still write and stay in touch.

My Mother's Eggplant

∼

VIJAYA BODACH

I believe in eggplant. My mother's eggplant.

Although I'd been fixing eggplant for many years, I didn't stumble across my mother's eggplant until my husband bought a ceramic barbecue. One evening, I handed over a shiny, purple eggplant for him to roast over the coals.

After the eggplant cooled off, I peeled the blackened skin, then mashed the pulp. I fried onions, garlic, chili peppers, turmeric, and cumin seeds. My big fancy kitchen took on the aroma of the tiny kitchen I had known as a child in India. I added the mashed eggplant along with finely chopped tomatoes and cilantro. At the very end, I added a dollop of creamy yogurt. It wasn't until supper, when I finally had a bite of the eggplant with my rice, that I started crying.

"What's the matter?" asked my husband. My small children looked worried.

"It's my mother's eggplant," I stuttered, tears streaming down my face. "It's my mother's eggplant."

"Really?" asked my four-year-old son.

I nodded my head. "She would love it if she were here with us today," I sobbed.

I missed my mother so much. She had died over twenty years ago, but at that moment I was missing her as though she'd only just left this world. I wished she were at our kitchen table, telling us family stories, enjoying the food that I had prepared.

My husband rubbed my back until the wracking subsided. The children ate their supper of Tandoori chicken, peas, rice, and yogurt. And I began to eat, slowly, with stories tumbling out of my mouth. "We were so poor growing up in India that we used our gas stove only for boiling water. We cooked our food on hot coals in a tiny chula, a barbecue smaller than even the baby Green Egg we take camping."

Some of my tears were from missing my mother. And some were because of the sudden realization that my son and daughter will never know her. I spooned a tiny bit of eggplant into my son's mouth. "Too spicy, Mommy," he said. He took several big gulps of milk. I held back giving a taste of it to my two-year-old daughter, who still enjoyed only completely plain food.

Both my children are in school now. They eat a wide variety of foods. They adore American hamburgers with a crisp vegetable platter. They love a Thai-style chicken-noodle soup. They gobble up South Indian rice crepes dipped in spicy lentil soup. And they eat my mother's eggplant with rice, reluctantly, just as I ate it unenthusiastically as a child. All these foods are served with stories, some of them breathing life into my mother.

I imagine my grown children might one day bring home a shiny eggplant, roast it over hot coals, and carefully season it. They'll remember to add a dollop of yogurt just before serving. And I believe they'll remember me, my mother, and my mother's eggplant.

VIJAYA BODACH is a scientist turned writer. She shares her love of food and cooking, inextricably linked to her mother, who could make even tea and rotis into a feast. Ms. Bodach encourages others to share family recipes and stories to help keep beloved dead alive in their hearts. To learn more about her, visit www.vijayabodach.com.

Dancing to the Music

AMANDA JOSEPH-ANDERSON

A multitude of ornate squares decorated a hunter-green carpeted floor. The Beatles and a few other notable artists were strung out in no particular order. I studied the album art, fascinated by the pictures and stories they told. I can recall creating my own dialogue for Sergeant Pepper's Lonely Hearts Club Band to better understand the meaning and purpose behind such flamboyant attire. What a necessary mess my mother and I had made.

This cyclical game we had played many times before. We would pull out all of my mother's old vinyl and designate a playlist. I picked mostly by the album's pictures, my mother by an artist's credibility and sound. I was a young child at the time; I didn't understand the dynamics of music.

The excitement and anticipation would build as the automatic arm positioned itself above a disk of splendor. The silver Pioneer would belt out sounds from the heavens. We then interlocked hands and twirled. Life would be forgotten in this world of ours. Our feet didn't stop until we paid homage to each tune. At no other time in my life can I remember such bliss and happiness.

I would always catch my mother turning the music up louder when she wanted to sing, in order to drown out her own voice. Nevertheless, I heard it, and it was beautiful.

She created beauty with such ease, just like those moments.

We would fade into our world for several hours. We ignored all the outside distractions. Our philosophy encouraged others to join us, or leave us alone. We were usually left alone. We danced like tribesmen waiting for the rain.

It took me years to realize the ulterior motives behind our musical endeavors. Of course my mother was very interactive with me when I was young. I have many fond memories of studying, playing games, and talking about fantasy worlds of dragons and fairies with her. But listening to music seemed to be her choice of play.

When we listened to music, I caught my mother in pure nostalgia. As we danced she would share fond moments of her life. It would almost bring her to tears. Reminiscing was always difficult for her because she had come from a happier place.

We always struggled as a family. My father was a verbally abusive alcoholic who favored breaking our spirits every time he drank. This was the "outside world" and the "distractions" that we would drown out with music.

My mother tried to instill in me the same happiness that she had been so accustomed to in her earlier years. She protected me and found a means of escape from the ugliness of our reality. And with the sounds of her music, she preserved my psychological well-being as well.

I realize now that our hours playing records and dancing together were more than just playtime—they bonded us and made us stronger than ever. And in so doing, I believe my mother made our love never ending, just like the infinite circle of an old LP.

AMANDA JOSEPH-ANDERSON is an elementary school teacher in Jenkins, Kentucky, where she lives with her mother, husband, and daughter. After becoming a mother herself, Ms. Joseph-Anderson feels blessed to have such a wonderful mother as a role model for raising her own little girl.

The Flaw-Free Body

KIKKI SHORT

I believe in teaching my daughter to love her body.

I think every kid starts out loving her body, reveling in each new trick it can perform, from learning to crawl to doing the hokey-pokey. Somewhere along the way, however, I've seen girls lose that joy and instead start seeing their bodies as imperfect machines that must constantly be improved and combed over for defects.

I want to positively shape my little girl's future by turning off the flaw finder in my own head, showing her I have a great body because it works—I can walk, bike, dance, and even run if something truly frightening is chasing me.

When my son pinches the fat on the back of my arm as I hold him on my hip, I remind myself that these arms can carry him for hours if they have to, they can swing my daughter up in the air, and they can do the knick-knack-paddy-whack-give-a-dog-a-bone with the best of them. This body walked me through the theater and into the practice room where I met my husband. This body carried two kids through full pregnancies before turning them out only when each was complete. This body has been known to get down, get funky, and even get the lead out. I love my body, and I want my daughter to see her body in the same way.

This doesn't mean that I have a so-called perfect body, and I'm *not* about to relate my hard-fought battle to return to fitness, turning my flabby parts into steel, feeling the burn, and strengthening my core. If you look at me, I think you could tell that my stomach muscles have gotten the kind of stretching that only pregnancy could possibly allow. Who wouldn't love to have zero cellulite and sculpted abs? I'm not immune to the shocking postpregnancy images of celebrities where only their lips seem to have gotten any bigger. But I am not a movie star surrounded by a phalanx of personal trainers. Right now I spend my time making models of the solar system or baking cakes with my daughter. My son is just learning to walk, and I spend my days keeping up with my kids, not going to the gym.

I never moan about the clear effects gravity has on breasts that are done breastfeeding; I've lived in my body, and I'm not ashamed of being thirty-seven or of having had two kids. In front of the mirror I say, "Check out my muscle-y arms!" or "I can stand on my toes!" I feel proud each time my daughter watches me get dressed and I don't say, "Does this make me look fat?" I show my daughter the wonders of skipping rope, the joys of hopping, and the elation of flying around like a scary pterodactyl.

I believe a healthy body is a treasure to celebrate.

KIKKI SHORT lives with her husband, two kids, one turtle, and one bearded dragon in New York. She teaches kids with learning disabilities.

Some Things to Know
About Your Mother

∽

ANNE DONAHUE

I believe a girl should know her mother. I mean really know her. On the highway, does she drive in the right-hand lane or the left? When she was a little girl, what did she hang on her bedroom wall? What really makes her laugh? How does she handle a bad day? Does she like to dance?

I lost my mother to colon cancer when I was five. She was forty-two. I do not know these things about my mother. I could ask; I have a wonderful father and five older siblings who had the honor of knowing her much longer than I did. But I'm Irish. If you are Irish, you may know what I mean. I don't tend to ask, and almost thirty years later, my mother's early death is still a very painful subject for me. But I have my assumptions, gleaned from years of careful listening. She was something of a cynic, like me, with a sharp wit. She was quick to laugh. She had a soft spot for children. She loved to read and write. She was loved by many, and we will always miss her.

At thirty-four, I just gave birth to my first baby. Grace, I am your mother. You are stuck with me. By the time you want to know these things about me, you may not think I am so cool anymore. Or, God forbid, I am not here to tell you. But I will be here. If it means a colonoscopy every month for the rest of my life, I will be here. But in case you don't ask, there are some small things about me you should know, if you should ever wonder.

So, I have a weakness for goofy-looking creatures. I know it's sappy, but after loving E.T. since I was a kid, I finally adopted our pug. It was the closest I could get.

My bedroom posters? They included E.T., Duran Duran, and Robert Parrish of the '84 Celtics.

I've always wondered what my mother found funny. For me, animals in human clothing always do the trick: a dog in a coat, a cat in a pillbox hat, or a chimp in a three-piece suit.

For the record, U2 is the best band on earth. This is not a matter for debate; it's the truth.

I always drive in the right-hand lane. You should know that your mother is a terrible driver. I am best off in the backseat with my eyes closed.

Last, if you're in a bad mood, try marching in place vigorously. I'm convinced marching always makes you feel better. It's simply impossible to feel anxious while marching.

Dear Grace, as long as I am here, please ask me anything, anytime. I believe a girl should know her mother.

ANNE DONAHUE is an online media director at a private investment firm. She lives in Westwood, Massachusetts, with her husband and now two daughters, Grace and Eve. They might want to know that their mother has a picture of a chimpanzee in a three-piece suit on her desk at work.

A Sacred Gift

ALICE ROCHE CODY

Six years ago, at sixteen weeks pregnant, I visited my doctor for a routine checkup. During the sonogram, he couldn't find my baby's heartbeat. It felt as though mine had stopped beating also.

I was blindsided by a grief so strong and powerful. People say that what doesn't kill you makes you stronger. This grief nearly broke my back. I endured a surgery. I saw specialists. No one could tell me why I lost my baby. I slipped into depression. The grief was like a full-time job. I couldn't leave it.

Our two-year-old son, Sean, kept me going. I got up every day for him. Sometimes I didn't make it farther than the living room couch. He drove toy trucks up and down my body. When I cried, he grabbed tissues and hugged me tight.

People dismissed my loss, saying it was God's will. I doubted that God sat up in heaven and decided to take my baby. I didn't believe God had a plan. I believed in the randomness of the universe.

People told me to be thankful for Sean. To focus on him, not my loss. I was grateful for Sean from the moment he was born. But I still grieved for my baby, and it took a long time. I felt that I couldn't even do grief right.

People said that in time I would find meaning in my loss, that it would transform me. This proved true. The private grief that I carried taught me not to run from the pain of others, as many did with me. It gave me courage.

Two years later, my husband and I were blessed with another son, Christopher. I started to put our loss in a different place. If our second baby had lived, we might not be holding our beloved son. Maybe God did have a plan.

Above all, grief has made me a better mother. I celebrate my children. I hug my sons and tell them I love them all day long. We dance to Christmas carols in the summer. We bang drums and sing Springsteen songs. We read together. We rake leaves. We bake cookies. And when a bowl of melted chocolate falls to the floor, I try not to get angry. We laugh, clean up, and start over.

I believe that motherhood is a sacred gift. I am careful with my children. I know life is fragile, and it takes all I have not to let fear stop me cold. When moms complain about their children, I want to yell, "Stop! Don't you realize the gift you have? Handle it with care."

Each year, we give to charity in honor of our baby. Quiet remembrances. My sorrow has now subsided, but sometimes I still yearn for that child. When that happens, I let myself cry and I welcome Sean's tissues. Then I hug my precious sons tightly.

After earning a master's degree in journalism from New York University, ALICE ROCHE CODY has worked as a reporter, writer, and media consultant. Simultaneously, she has navigated the joys and challenges of motherhood as she and her husband, Patrick, raise their two sons, Sean and Christopher, in Bernardsville, New Jersey. She draws on her previous professional and family adventures as she writes her first novel.

Motherhood Is Real

WENDY LAWRENCE

I believe in motherhood—that intangible and immortal connection. An untouchable idea forged by generations of mothers, all hugging, grasping, and holding on, I believe it powers us all.

Motherhood evolved from the first primordial soup, from shared mitochondria, from instinct encoded deep within DNA's coils. Motherhood is the definitive relation, the essential connection that informs all other connections. Connected to our mothers, we are linked to a past that is both evolutionary and personal.

My mom complimented me on my first basket in basketball, even though I scored it for the wrong team. Her belief in that basket powers my heart today as I—forever the girl running the twelve-minute mile—train for another triathlon, knowing that I will still be slow and not even considering that I should care. Her belief opens my lungs as I jump off the ledge of an established career to follow my dream of being a writer. With one compliment, my mom gave me the confidence to tempt failure. I still believe in those two points.

There are times when we don't believe in motherhood. I remember middle school, the first arguments I had with my mom, the first time I realized she could be wrong. My mother is not perfect, I thought, and the world stopped spinning for a minute. We believe and then we don't believe.

And then we believe again. When my high school dropped the speech and debate program, my mom co-coached the team with a teddy bear, as if anyone would have done the same. I believed in that teddy bear, but it didn't occur to me until many years later that my mother must have, too. An adult now, and a mother myself, I have a mini-epiphany: of course mothers must believe! Against all odds, they must believe.

To believe in what a mother can do is to stretch the imagination to a different world: to believe in humanity above all else, to believe in the power of love and hot soup, to believe in our own power to save the world. A child must believe strongly enough to hold on even when he doesn't want to. A mother must believe strongly enough to let go.

I remember the day she stopped breathing, the water running down my naked body as I showered in the next room. I remember feeling surprised somehow to be alive without her. Pouring her ashes into a painted box, burying her under the dandelions and California poppies. There was nothing more to touch. But I remember my belief solidifying. Motherhood was a real thing.

A mother's touch is your first reality: it's a hug. It's a grasping hand that drags you midtantrum across the grocery store. It's my mom holding me in a rocking chair, even though I know I'm too old. A mother's touch grounds you to your own life. It grounds me to the first thing I truly believed.

WENDY LAWRENCE is a writer, blogger, and educator who is now studying the other half of the motherhood equation with her two young sons and husband in Nashville, Tennessee. Previously, she worked with kids and their mothers as a middle school teacher and principal. She blogs on mothering and books at The Family That Reads Together and on parenting at Nashville Parent.

Miracle from Within

GEETA MAKER-CLARK, MD

For all of our greatest advances in medicine, the work of bringing a child into the world will always rest on the limbs, strength, and soul of the woman in its throes. It is epic, it is transformative, and it is as old as life itself. This precious event is often taken over by the medical world, and I believe we need to take it back.

I have no dark past with the medical profession that has embittered me. In fact, I am a physician. Delivering babies has been one of my greatest privileges, and I have never walked away from a single one, even after call nights that brought ten babies into my hands, without some humility and awe for what women can do. Of course, medical heroics are occasionally necessary, and many times I have felt the tension of getting a distressed baby out as fast as possible. Yet the truth is, I know that a woman possesses an instinctual knowledge of how to birth her baby, and that for all of my training and expertise, I do best by her when I let her connect with her own body and do the work she was meant to do.

I remember well when I began to realize that no one, not even the most wizened of obstetricians, knew more about birthing than the mother herself. It was the end of my residency—I had already accepted an obstetric fellowship and felt comfortable with my skills—when a physician I had barely worked with supervised me during a birth. I was sitting beside my patient, advising her on pushing positions, breathing techniques, and generally talking her through labor. This was my usual spiel, and I thought it was important. Everything I had been taught and had observed before that day had reinforced that for me. This physician quietly told me to stop talking, sit on my hands, and wait. With some difficulty, I complied for what seemed an eternity of silence, maybe about forty-five minutes, as the woman before me went deep within herself, into her own rhythm, and pushed her baby out with great effort and sound, but without instruction or intervention. I lifted her baby onto her chest and moved aside for the excited family to behold. I was humbled, and moved. No one had taught me that birthing is not an acquired skill, that it comes from within. I learned this again powerfully when I birthed my own three children.

After catching hundreds of babies and learning ways to do so from many physicians and midwives, when my time came I knew that I wanted that chance to find my own power. I chose midwives whom I knew I could trust if things went awry, and who would also honor my choice to follow my body and my baby's lead. To finally experience the intensity and pain and joy I had seen pass through other women was exhilarating. And I was able to birth in the way that I needed to when the waves of labor began. All three births were very different, though my daughters were both born in birthing tubs into the water, and my son at a hospital "on land."

There are few things that have been around since the beginning of time. Birth *is* the beginning of time. For me, it is a great metaphor for all that is still mysterious and magnificent in the world—all that exists before and above medicine's reach. I believe that through understanding the power and instinct that is so manifest in the event of birth, I can see the realization of my most far-flung ideas, for myself and for the world. Birth is an everyday miracle. And I believe that we are capable of such majesty, every day and in every way.

GEETA MAKER-CLARK, MD, is an integrative family physician, yogini, and mother living in Evanston, Illinois. She is passionate about dancing, using food as medicine, and living family life slowly. She lives in a brick bungalow with her husband, Todd, and her three children, Sahaara, Sachin, and Devika.

The Essential Gift of Childhood

MARLA ROSE

I believe in my three-year-old son, who is not in the 95th percentile of anything, who did not know his alphabet by his first birthday, who is struggling mightily with shoes and the potty and most social graces. He is truly mournful when leaves fall off the trees in autumn, and he is as gentle and weird and kind as I'd dreamed my child would be. He does not know a second language yet, but he has a magical belly laugh. I believe if I could play a recording of it to warring nations, he would be heralded as an international peacekeeper.

When I was a child in the 1970s, children were woefully unfashionable. Yet, in retrospect, that decade may have been the last time children were allowed some breathing space. We didn't have to dwell so much on adult preoccupations of trends, fashion, and getting ahead. We could just be children.

I'm not romanticizing my own childhood, because it could be such a brutal, scary time. In my youth, I learned about alcoholism, about mothers who cried themselves to sleep, and about the everyday cruelties classmates inflict on some of us. I do not see childhood in a sepia-toned, idealized way.

This is why I so fiercely guard my son's youth. In the years before we had hundreds of cable channels, and parents thought their newborns should be baby geniuses, negotiating the often pretty rugged terrain of childhood was our chief concern. I understand that the push for achievement and the pressures we face as parents can be overwhelming. But I believe that I would be robbing my child of an essential gift if I didn't nurture and protect his youth. The world of playtime and the outdoors is the best laboratory available to my son.

Last week, we were at the playground when I heard a freckled girl in pull-ups call out to her mother from the top of the slide, asking for juice. "Ask me again in French," said her mother. The girl complied with an impatient eye-roll. At that moment, all I could feel was worry for my child, who is still just getting his feet wet in English, scared that he'd be left behind.

But then I heard my son laughing. He was watching two squirrels chase each other up and down and around a maple tree. "Squirrels are silly," he said.

Motherhood is a state of always being vulnerable to our expectations and worries about our children. I know that at his core, my son is a happy, free-spirited boy having the childhood he deserves. When I am at my best, I know that there is absolutely nothing to worry about. So at that moment, I forgot about his French-speaking peer and picked my son up, nuzzling those delicious, satiny cheeks, and said "Yes, squirrels are silly."

I believe in the silliness of squirrels, I believe in my son, and I believe in his childhood.

MARLA ROSE is a freelance writer and aspiring novelist living with her family in Oak Park, Illinois.

Heaven Is Now

AMY MILLER

I have never climbed Mount Everest, surfed the shores of Peru, or cooked a twelve-course meal. But I have read my children a bedtime story, hugged my husband, and told my sister, "I love you." I live the best I can within each mundane, "everyday" day. I pour Cheerios for breakfast. Drive the carpool. Plan a birthday party. I do not yearn to meet the Dalai Lama nor covet the Pulitzer Prize. This I believe: if I live in the present, finding joy and peace in my daily life, I live fully. If I conduct myself with grace, I set an example for my children.

Where I grew up, parents let their kids wander. "Come home when the street lights go on," Mom said. We biked or roller-skated to the park and scooted home for dinner as the day cooled into evening. Our parents assumed we could get from the street to the table unharmed. Where I live today, we fear letting our children ride their bikes more than a block. The idea of my daughter walking home from school alone sends a shiver down my spine. What if she were kidnapped? Hit by a car?

My anxiety comes from reality. During my teens, a friend fell out of a moving pickup truck. A prankster, he thought it would be funny to stand up in the back. He did not survive the fall. Our small town grieved for this boy, so handsome, so golden, so young he had not graduated from high school. Here I sit, thirty years later, still mourning him. And I feel afraid.

How do we live our lives when we know death lurks around the corner? What motivates us to carry on despite devastating loss? This boy's parents provide great instruction. They tended their child's grave, marked his birthdays and anniversaries with flowers. They established a scholarship. They grieved openly and privately. Gradually, in bits and pieces, they soldiered on.

Until recently, my own life was as relatively peaceful as the bike rides of my youth. But whether we experience the death of a child or a shocking illness, at some point, the peace ends. At forty-four, I was diagnosed with advanced lung cancer. My daughters were five and eight at the time. After surgery, radiation, and chemotherapy, I still live with a chronic disease and ongoing treatment. We may close our eyes to the specter, the blob under the bed, the creature in the closet. The tragedy. But it is there.

Like my friend's parents, I too soldier on. I kiss my kids good-bye each morning, reasonably confident they will return safely. I help them master fourth-grade history and sixth-grade math, assuming they will grow up to graduate high school and go to college. I celebrate another birthday. Cook spaghetti for dinner. Scoop chocolate ice cream. Savor the sunset. Simply, I live. While I can imagine a utopia, I believe there is no heaven except the place we are right now.

AMY MILLER lives with her husband, daughters, and Wheaten terrier by the shore in Manhattan Beach, California. She grew up in Claremont, California. A graduate of UCLA, she enjoys walking on the beach, reading, and meditating.

Words Can Heal the Heart
of a Mother

∽

LYNDA SENTZ

As a writer I love words. There is nothing like turning a phrase that strikes a chord with a reader. It's an unexpected gift, and I love to be the giver. But one rainy, dank July day, I received the gift of five extraordinary words.

My son Tyler graduated from high school and walked away from an ROTC scholarship to go straight into the U.S. Army. I always knew he would enlist, but college first had always been the plan. But Tyler was in a hurry to serve, intent on starting at the bottom and working his way to the top on his own merit. Admirable, yes, but tell that to the heart of a mother.

The day I learned of his decision was the day the bottom fell out for me as a mother. After years of being the "decider" for my children, I felt I had failed as a parent. The next weeks were filled with dread of the future, like waiting for a funeral. The fear of what could happen to Tyler nearly crippled me. If screaming and crying could have prevented my son from going, he'd be with me still.

High school graduation came and went. I planned a celebration though my heart was absolutely, utterly broken. Next I planned a farewell gathering, going through the motions of letting go. The ties that bind were being crudely severed, inflicting the worst pain I had ever experienced as a mother. A verse of scripture from the Gospel of Matthew haunted me: "In Rama was there a voice heard, lamentation and weeping, and great mourning, Rachel weeping for her children and would not be comforted because they are not." There was no consoling me.

There were parties for the children of our friends and relatives to celebrate their bright futures and to wish them well. Imagine rubbing salt in an open wound. I wished their joy could be mine. At one party, I ran into an acquaintance from years ago. Catching up on our lives included my sharing my son's choice to serve his country. When Tyler arrived, I introduced him, and it happened. My friend spoke those five words:

"Thank you for your service."

The words came easily, with sincerity, kindness, and tremendous respect. I was astonished, speechless even. Of all the things people said of my son's decision, "thank you" hadn't been among them. It was a moment in my child's life that will stay with me forever. In my heart, it ranks with other big moments I've shared with Tyler—his birth, first step, first day of school—his first thank you as a soldier.

His departure for the Army was terrible, and the days since then have been brutal. Even so, I want to thank you, my precious son, for your service. To all who have served and their families: thank you for your service, your sacrifice.

Words have great power—they can inform, persuade, cause great hurt. I believe words can also heal the broken heart of a mother.

Writer and teacher LYNDA SENTZ is the mother of four sons, two of whom serve in the military today. She lives in Hamburg, New York, where she and her husband wait for their sons' phone calls and letters.

The Second-Hardest Job

TINA BOSCHA

I believe that stepparents have the second-hardest job there is, second only—this is a close second—to parenting.

It's hard to say when I became a stepparent. Was it the time when I, not Dad, was nudged awake at 3:00 AM by the youngest when she felt nauseous? Was it the first time I was called "Mom" by "accident"? Or was it just a few weeks ago, when my husband and I officially married? It wasn't the latter; I was Stepmom long before that. But the exact moment can't be pinpointed. Stepparents don't have the miraculous day of childbirth. Instead, they have the initial awkward meeting, where the kids avoid eye contact and stare all at the same time, and friends call immediately afterward to ask, "How'd it go?"

People say my situation is lucky, but I think that's a response to the stereotype of stepparents as selfish, uninterested, and threatened, or stepkids as hostile and sullen. I have a great relationship with my stepdaughters, who call me both Tina and Mom, and we've decided that whatever name comes out first is okay. I have a warm relationship with their mother, who is always Mommy, but who respects the importance of my role. She calls us a team; together with my husband, we say we coparent.

This doesn't mean it's easy. It's weird sometimes. When my husband went out of town on a weekend that was "ours," I wondered, do I still have the kids? Then I wondered, if he dies, what happens to me? What happens to Stepmom? Questions like these affirm my belief that stepparenting is extraordinarily difficult. Stepparenting's role and expectations are amorphous. I constantly wonder about the intensity of my feelings—love, fear, anger, frustration—and I ask myself, what if these girls were biologically mine? How intense would my feelings be then? Sometimes, I question if I don't feel enough. I've decided to accept that these questions don't have answers. And in the end, I did have the kids that weekend.

I wipe away snot, worry about calcium intake, buy them new shoes every other week. I call in sick when the youngest has the flu again. I raise my voice and make them fold their laundry. I get annoyed at too many questions and wish they'd go away, and five minutes later, smile at the energy they give our home with the silly dances they choreograph and the extraordinarily strange ways they put clothes together.

I may not know just when I became a stepparent, but I do know that I will be one for the rest of my life. I am forever changed. I believe that my role as Stepmom is ill-defined and important and that the teenage years, just two years away, will try my patience in ways I can't yet imagine.

Bring it on.

TINA BOSCHA is a stepmom, wife, writer, and teacher living in Brownsville, Oregon. To keep her sanity during the teenage years, she sews and knits. She recently published her first novel, *River in the Sea*, based on her mother's teenage years during World War II.

Bessie Mae: Nobody Famous

MICHAEL TAYLOR

I believe the best heroes are the ones who have not been publicly recognized. They are someone's hero simply by living their life as usual, not necessarily striving for anything particular outside of survival. They are everyday folks.

Therefore, my greatest hero definitely isn't a celebrity or someone who lived a rags-to-riches story. As a matter of fact, this person isn't a hero at all. She is a heroine: my mother. She is known by the simple appellation of Bessie Mae, and she has been my greatest source of inspiration.

A brief glance into this extraordinary woman's life makes it clear. As part of the last wave of people leaving the South during the Black Diaspora, we settled in small town Bloomington, Illinois. My mother was married to a man who pledged his allegiance to vodka practically every day. As Mother explained to us later in life, she simply didn't want us growing up exposed to an alcoholic. So, one day she packed up her seven kids in an old brown Dodge station wagon, hitched a U-haul trailer to it, and headed back down south to Montgomery, Alabama.

She had every excuse to give up or even to turn to alcohol or drugs, but she did not, though the entire deck was stacked against her. At five foot three, she was a black woman of small stature, with no college education in a southern cesspool of racism in the mid-1970s. But for her, giving up was not an option. She did whatever she had to do to survive as a single parent and to successfully raise all her children to adulthood.

By high school I had started to sense that my mother had accomplished something amazing as a single parent. Then, when I was seventeen years old, I signed up for the Marine Corps. The day I left for basic training, my mother told me, a skinny, nervous black kid, four simple words: "Just do your best." That expression may be a cliché, but coming from her it has given me a lifetime of powerful inspiration.

I've had my share of ups and downs in my life, from military service to working as a border agent in Southern

California to a three-year jail sentence for taking bribes from smugglers. Through every obstacle I encountered, I would think to myself, "If Mother overcame her challenges, I have no excuse not to do the same." The more I matured, the more I admired her for what she had achieved.

Things are going well for me since my release from prison. I graduated from community college with highest honors, and now I'm a student at Columbia University. Every step of the way, I have been fueled by the inspiration of my mother—my hero. I have never given up. I have tried to do my best. And I owe it all to Bessie Mae, a black woman who never gave an inch in the face of life's unforgiving challenges.

MICHAEL TAYLOR is a professional archaeologist and a student at Columbia University in New York City. He is finishing a degree in archaeological anthropology. Mr. Taylor volunteers at the Fortune Society, a nonprofit organization that helps former inmates successfully reenter society.

Pieces of Me

KIMBERLY TREVISANI

My friend Pam died of cancer last December. She was thirty-five, happily married with two young children. The illness spread quickly, poisoning her body but never her spirit. Although cancer robbed my friend of her life, it taught me to appreciate the little moments of my own.

One fall day, Pam talked about her seven-year-old daughter, who had just learned to ride her bicycle without training wheels. Her face fell when she said, "I missed it." The silence in the hospital room spoke volumes. I didn't need her to say any more. As a mother, I instantly understood the complexity of her simple, poignant statement.

What she said struck a chord within me so deep that it still resonates today.

"I missed it because I'm in here. I can't be a mom anymore. I won't see my children grow. I'm going to miss so much more."

This spring, my son rode his bike for the first time. As I watched his clumsy initial attempts transform into confidence, tears welled in my eyes. I stopped jogging alongside him and watched the distance between us grow. All I could think of were Pam's words. I tried to burn his image into my mind to make sure I wouldn't forget what he looked like. And I cried. I cried for my friend and all that she will never witness. I cried for her daughter and son, who didn't have a mom waiting at the end of the road. I cried for her husband, who will experience these moments alone.

As my son turned the corner and came back to me, a funny thing happened. I wiped my tears away and smiled. I needed to enjoy this moment because Pam was never able to. She would want me to cheer him on and wave my arms like a lunatic as he looped around the block. I needed to remember it for her, not despite her.

How often do I get caught up in the small things in life? Packing lunches, making doctor's appointments, and folding laundry. Some call them chores, but now I believe they are what make a life. These small details used to seem endless and overwhelming, but now it's okay.

I want to be there to give my kids a bath after a day of playing outside in the mud. I want to scrub the grass stains out of their worn-out, threadbare jeans. I want to rush through the aisles of a grocery store looking for a last-minute dinner ingredient. I want to cram a haircut in between soccer games and kissing a scraped knee. I want to scramble for a babysitter so that my husband and I can finally have a "date night."

I appreciate my chaos because it's mine. These details are the pieces of me that make up my life. My moments. I don't want to miss them.

KIMBERLY TREVISANI lives in Whitesboro, New York, with her husband and two sons. She has been a high school English teacher for thirteen years, and she has given her seniors the *This I Believe* essay assignment for the last three years. Her students always want to know if she herself has written one, and now she can say that she has.

Am I Doing This Right?

JEANA LEE TAHNK

Am I doing this right?

As a mom, that is a question I ask myself on a daily basis. Whether it's disciplining tactics or sleep training or wondering if the organic cheez-puffs are really *that* much better for my kids, motherhood has been a type of training in progress for me; I learn as I go along. Life as a mom and CEO of a household is challenging, and between caring for two young kids, cultivating a successful career, managing schedules, and running a home, the question always remains . . . am I doing this right?

My endless struggle to find balance between my work life and my home life is difficult to navigate. That, on top of wondering if I'm parenting in a way that my kids will need therapy for, is what makes questioning if I'm doing it "right" all the more salient. While I immensely value and recognize my contribution to my family as a mom, it is important to me to contribute to myself through my career as well. And seeking this kind of balance has presented its fair share of obstacles along the way.

Once, on a day when my kids were home, I had to participate in an important client conference call. (Important calls and kids at home don't complement each other that well, as you can imagine.) In the midst of the discussion, I actually had to run, yes run, down the hall away from my toddler daughter so that her high-pitched screeches wouldn't filter through the phone and be heard by the CEO, president, and VP of marketing on the other end. While I sat breathless behind the bed, literally hiding from her, I rushed through my talking points in a harried whisper so that I could retreat back into my "safe" mode on mute. The memory of that makes me laugh now, but at that moment, fleeing from my child was the choice I had to make.

I've learned over the years that this is what motherhood is about. It's about the moment-to-moment. It's about making the decisions that I think are right at the time and believing in them. I know I'll look back and have regrets about certain ways I handled situations, or things I could have said differently, but it is in the collection of these moments that I define myself as a mom, a wife, and a woman.

There are so many joys and challenges that come with being a mom, and despite my constant questioning, I know I'll never have all the answers. What I do know is that the decisions I make for my children are always with their best interests at heart and that "right" means many different things at many different times. With that in mind, I can have the confidence and believe, yes, I *am* doing this right.

JEANA LEE TAHNK is a writer and regular contributor to the Huffington Post, *Parenting* magazine, Mashable, Cool Mom Tech, and others, exploring parenting, technology, and the intersection of the two. She lives in the Boston area with her husband, their two young kids, and dog.

How to Write Your Own
This I Believe Essay

We invite you to contribute to this project by writing and submitting your own statement of personal belief. We understand how challenging this is—it requires such intimacy that you may find it difficult to begin. To guide you through this process, we offer these suggestions:

Tell a story. Be specific. Take your belief out of the ether and ground it in the events of your life. Your story need not be heartwarming or gut-wrenching—it can even be funny—but it should be real. Consider moments when your belief was formed, tested, or changed. Make sure your story ties to the essence of your daily life philosophy and to the shaping of your beliefs.

Be brief. Your statement should be between 350 and 500 words. The shorter length forces you to focus on the belief that is central to your life.

Name your belief. If you can't name it in a sentence or two, your essay might not be about belief. Rather than writing a list, consider focusing on one core belief.

Be positive. Say what you do believe, not what you don't believe. Avoid statements of religious dogma, preaching, or editorializing.

Be personal. Make your essay about you; speak in the first person. Try reading your essay aloud to yourself several times, and each time edit it and simplify it until you find the words, tone, and story that truly echo your belief and the way you speak.

Please submit your completed essay to the *This I Believe* organization by visiting the website, www.thisibelieve.org. We are eager for your contribution.

ACKNOWLEDGMENTS

First and foremost, we offer our deepest gratitude to the essayists who contributed their work to this book. We honor their willingness to express the things that matter most and to share their stories in this collection.

In reviving *This I Believe*, we are forever grateful to Casey Murrow, Keith Wheelock, and Margot Wheelock Schlegel, the children of the *This I Believe* radio program creators Edward R. Murrow and Ward Wheelock. Our project continues to be guided by Edward R. Murrow and his team, which preceded us in the 1950s: Gladys Chang Hardy, Reny Hill, Donald J. Merwin, Edward P. Morgan, Raymond Swing, and Ward Wheelock.

Special thanks go to Jay Allison and Viki Merrick at Atlantic Public Media in Woods Hole, Massachusetts, for editing and producing the essay "Some Things to Know About Your Mother."

Our deepest and sincerest thanks go to Laura Coons for her expert editorial assistance. Her insights, organizational skills, and constant cheerful attitude were of immense help in bringing this book to life.

We are truly and deeply grateful for our This I Believe board of directors, who give their time and talents to strengthening our organization. Thank you to Marty Bollinger, John Y. Brown III, Mark Contreras, James Guerra, Jerry Howe, David Langstaff, Lynn Amato Madonna, and Declan Murphy.

Our most recent on-air home has been the *Bob Edwards Show* on Sirius XM Satellite Radio and *Bob Edwards Weekend* on Public Radio International. Our heartfelt thanks go to Bob Edwards and his wonderful staff: Steve Lickteig, Geoffrey Redick, Ed McNulty, Ariana Pekary, Shelley Tillman, Dan Bloom, Andy Kubis, Chad Campbell, and Cristy Meiners. At Sirius XM, we thank Jeremy Coleman, Frank Raphael, and Kevin Straley.

We also express our gratitude to everyone at NPR, which aired our radio series for the first four years, especially Jay Kernis, Stacey Foxwell, and Robert Spier, who were passionate and steadfast supporters.

The comprehensive website for *This I Believe* (www .thisibelieve.org) was built by Dennis Whiteman at Fastpipe Media, and was designed by LeapFrog Interactive with help from Chris Enander of TBD Design. Our iPhone app was cocreated by Dennis along with Wayne Walrath at Acme Technologies.

The creation of this book was immeasurably aided by our agent, Andrew Blauner, of Blauner Books Literary Agency. We are so fortunate to continue to have his able services and his unwavering support.

Our publisher, Jossey-Bass, and its parent company, John Wiley & Sons, have been tremendously supportive of our recent publishing activities. We are deeply indebted to editor Kate Bradford and her entire team for their passion and professionalism. We are deeply grateful especially for the skills and support of Nana Twumasi, Carol Hartland, and Michele D. Jones.

And, finally, we thank the tens of thousands of individuals who have accepted our invitation to write and share their own personal statements of belief. This book contains but a fraction of the many thoughtful and inspiring essays that have been submitted to our project, and we are grateful for them all. We invite you to join this group by writing your own *This I Believe* essay and submitting it to us via our website, www.thisibelieve.org. You will find instructions in the Appendix of this book on how to do so.